# Literacy as a Moral Imperative

# Culture and Education Series

Series Editors: Henry A. Giroux, Pennsylvania State University
Joe L. Kincheloe, Pennsylvania State University

*Race-ing Representation: Voice, History, and Sexuality*
    edited by Kostas Myrsiades and Linda Myrsiades, 1998
*Between the Masks: Resisting the Politics of Essentialism*
    by Diane DuBose Brunner
*The Mouse That Roared: Disney and the End of Innocence*, 1999
    by Henry Giroux
*Schooling as a Ritual Performance: Toward a Political Economy of Educational Symbols and Gestures*, 1999
    by Peter McLaren
*Literacy as a Moral Imperative: Facing the Challenges of a Pluralistic Society*
    by Rebecca Powell

*Forthcoming:*

*Cutting Class: Social Class and Education*
    edited by Joe L. Kincheloe and Shirley R. Steinberg
*None of the Above: Behind the Myth of Scholastic Aptitude, Updated Edition*
    by David Owen with Marilyn Doerr
*Pierre Bourdieu: Fieldwork in Art, Literature, and Culture*
    edited by Imre Szeman and Nicholas Brown
*Between Hope and Despair: Pedagogy and the Remembrance of Historical Trauma*
    edited by Roger I. Simon, Sharon Rosenberg, and Claudia Eppert
*The Ethics of Writing: Derrida, Deconstruction, and Pedagogy*
    by Peter Trifonas

# Literacy as a Moral Imperative

## *Facing the Challenges of a Pluralistic Society*

REBECCA POWELL

ROWMAN & LITTLEFIELD PUBLISHERS, INC.
*Lanham • Boulder • New York • Oxford*

ROWMAN & LITTLEFIELD PUBLISHERS, INC.

Published in the United States of America
by Rowman & Littlefield Publishers, Inc.
4720 Boston Way, Lanham, Maryland 20706
http://www.rowmanlittlefield.com
12 Hid's Copse Road
Cumnor Hill, Oxford OX2 9JJ, England

Excerpts from:
  *To Know as We Are Known*: Copyright © 1983, 1993 by Parker J. Palmer. Reprinted by
    permission of HarperCollins Publishers, Inc.
*Living between the Lines*. Reprinted by permission of Lucy McCormick Calkins with
    Shelley Harwayne. Published by Heinemann, a division of Reed Elsevier Inc.,
    Portsmouth, NH, 1991.
"Focus: A Ride on the Mantrip" by Carol Stumbo: From *Hands On*, 1987. Reprinted with
    permission from The Foxfire Fund, Inc.; Mountain City, GA. Copyright © 1987.
*Teaching to Transgress* by bell hooks: Copyright © 1994 Gloria Watkins. Reproduced by
    permission of Routlege, Inc.
*Will My Name Be Shouted Out?* by Stephen O'Connor. Copyright © 1996. Reprinted by
    permission of Simon & Schuster, Inc.

British Library Cataloguing in Publication Information Available

**Library of Congress Cataloging-in-Publication Data**

Powell, Rebecca, 1949-
    Literacy as a moral imperative : facing the challenges of a pluralistic society /
Rebecca Powell.
        p.   cm. -- (Culture and education series)
    Includes bibliographical references (p. ) and index.
    ISBN 0-8476-9458-5 (alk. paper). -- ISBN 0-8476-9459-3 (pbk. ; alk. paper)
    1. Literacy--Social aspects--United States. 2. Moral education--United States. 3.
Critical pedagogy--United States. 4. Education--Aims and objectives--United States.
I. Title. II. Series.
LC151.P69  1999
302.2'244--dc21                                                                99-15039
                                                                                CIP

Printed in the United States of America

⊖™ The paper used in this publication meets the minimum requirements of American
National Standard for Information Sciences—Permanence of Paper for Printed Library
Materials, ANSI/NISO Z39.48–1992.

This book is dedicated to my son, Justin Matthew Eller (5/10/81–4/11/93), whose life and untimely death provided the inspiration for this book. *I will love you forever.*

# Contents

# Acknowledgments

No work is ever the result of a single individual, and I wish to thank all of those who have guided my work over the years and who have encouraged me to write this book. First, thanks go to my former teachers who were instrumental in developing my writing ability, and especially to my former mentor, Christine Pappas, who helped me to see myself as a writer. Special recognition also goes to Diane Campbell, Carolyn Panofsky, and Linda Spears-Bunton, who have spent countless hours reading drafts of this and other texts. I am particularly grateful to the women and men of color who have chosen to be my friends, for through their willingness to share their often painful stories, they have given me a glimpse of what life is like in this nation for those who do not look like me. Last but certainly not least, I thank the members of my family: my parents, who provided me with love and security so that I could pursue my life's work; my husband Jerry for his enduring patience and support; my son Ryan and stepson Michael for their encouragement; and my son Justin, whose death at a young age provided me with the passion that I needed to write about something that really matters.

# Introduction

Contemporary rhetoric is filled with images of morality that dictate how we are to act, behave, and believe—images that implore us to become good citizens, to contribute to the national interest, to be productive workers within a competitive capitalistic system. Morality in this sense involves an obligation to follow the rules, to obey the laws of the land, and to do our part in maintaining a safe society. Certainly, few would disagree that we ought to act in ways that respect the rights of others and that contribute to a state of honesty and decency. Yet I would argue that this is a minimalist conception of morality that does little to address the serious flaws of American society. Indeed, its popular appeal undoubtedly evolves from the fact that it demands little of us as individuals, either in terms of critical thought or sacrificial action.

Rather, the image of morality that frames this volume goes beyond a paternalistic ethic of benevolence, beyond neoconservative notions of goodness, beyond contemporary portrayals of integrity and virtue. It is an image that takes us into the political domain—a domain of privilege and power, of poverty and subjugation, of hopelessness and acquiescence. It is within this political domain that our conceptions of literacy have evolved, and thus it is within this domain that we must interrogate our instructional practices. As a system for constituting our individual and collective voices, literacy is caught in the web of social stratification and control; glaringly absent in most schools and classrooms is a discourse that seeks to realize the democratic tenets of freedom and justice for all. Hence, our perceptions of literacy and the ways that it is taught in schools militate against the realization of a moral, democratic vision—a vision that is driven by a quest for equity and is sustained by a culture of care. This volume is about values, power, and the teaching of literacy in a pluralistic society. It is a book that examines the sober reality of oppression and the forces of hegemony that sustain it. It is a book that confronts the tragedy of hopelessness and the system of privilege that perpetuates it. Finally, it is a book that advocates the recovery of democratic principles that can unite our shattered society, a book that endorses a counterhegemonic language of emancipation and empowerment. In this sense, then, it is fundamentally a book about the moral decisions we face as educators—decisions about what to teach and how to teach it, about the goals we establish for ourselves and for our students, about the role we play in perpetuating images of cultural inferiority and superiority, and about whose interests we ultimately serve.

Our society is ravaged by social ills of enormous magnitude: racism, violence, and economic deprivation. These problems can only be overcome through the development of a collective social consciousness and a commitment to a moral vision. At the same time, most teachers honestly believe that they act in moral ways in the goals they set for their students. Their professed aims are to help all students to become productive members of the workforce, to enable all students to have choices in their lives, to prepare them to be effective citizens. These are commendable goals. Rarely, however, do teachers interrogate the ideological forces that shape these goals and that define their role as educators. Thus, while teachers may have moral intentions, they operate within a system that often prohibits these intentions from being realized—a system that mystifies the meritocratic function of literacy and schooling, that encourages individual versus collaborative response, and that immobilizes us to act in transformative ways.

In fact, it seems that we consciously strive to avoid serious debate in classrooms, as well as in our teacher education programs. We continue to operate as if the good life as it is defined within contemporary society is unproblematic and is equally available to all, as if our current ways of looking at the world are neutral, as if our present definitions of achievement are rational and unbiased. Indeed, it is interesting (as well as revealing) that in a society that purports to offer freedom and justice for all and that cherishes equality and individual rights, critical dialogue on such topics is regarded as extraneous to the educational enterprise. Despite our pride in existing as a democracy—a form of governance where active participation is essential and debate is encouraged—a serious examination of differences is seen as a threat rather than as a necessity.

Our instructional practices—indeed, even our efforts at educational reform—reflect these conserving tendencies. Efforts are made to upgrade teacher preparation programs so that teachers might be trained in all of the latest teaching methods. Policies are established so that students remain on task for more minutes during the day, hours during the week, and days during the year. Achievement tests that purport to be unbiased are increasingly being used for purposes of accountability and hence continue to drive curriculum decisions. Despite recent postmodern discourse that validates alternative ways of knowing, modernist, technical assumptions about teaching and learning prevail in discussions of schooling—assumptions where teachers are seen as workers/managers, students are seen as products, and the state functions as overseer of the entire educational enterprise.

Consistent with postmodern thought, recent theories about literacy and language suggest that teachers and students bring multiple interpretations to texts, and that language learning is an active, dynamic process requiring authentic interaction in genuine social contexts. Such theories challenge technicist notions that regard language as a mere conduit and the assessment of that knowledge as a neutral endeavor. In fact, as I argue throughout this book, the ways in which literacy is defined both in society and in our educational institutions is highly political. This fact, I would suggest, can no longer be ignored.

As a former classroom teacher, I have not always recognized the nonneutrality of literacy instruction. Educated within a system that legitimated my whiteness and that endorsed my ways of seeing the world, I was committed to teaching my students to adapt to mainstream culture so that they might succeed in society. As a public school teacher, I basically fit into the system and was regarded by both parents and administrators to be a good teacher. I followed the teachers' manuals, managed the classroom effectively, and attempted to provide a warm and inviting environment for my elementary students. We assumed traditional roles; I taught, and my students learned. It has only been recently, however, that I realized that what I taught and what they learned was knowledge defined and legitimized largely by those outside of the institution and, more importantly, outside of their lives.

I recall Teresa, a second grade Anglo student from a lower-class community, whose mother warned me never to touch her child, for she had been physically (and psychologically) bruised by teachers in previous years. Teresa was a quiet girl, always willing to comply with my wishes and demands. I often wondered what would prompt a teacher to punish her so severely. Over the years, I also have come to realize that, while I may not have further damaged her, I also offered her very little that would enrich her life.

Then there was James, a tall and burly African American fifth grader, who would spend what seemed like an endless amount of time in the library just to escape my remedial reading classroom. Although he felt comfortable enough to prop his feet up on his desk in my class, I was not comfortable enough to allow him to do so. And although I gave him the freedom—at least some of the time—to read books of his choice, there were very few books in the school library's collection that related to his life.

I also recall Damon, an eight-year-old child of African American descent whose small size made him appear to be two years younger, and whose reading level was lower still. I recall my frustration as I attempted to teach Damon to read, using basal readers and the language experience approach. I now realize that the language and experiences I gave to Damon were someone else's, not his—the language and experiences that, from my position of White privilege, I presumed he needed in order to succeed.

For these and other students, what I offered was a literacy not of hope, but of alienation; not of empowerment, but of control. What they needed, and what I was ill-prepared to give, was a literacy of promise and possibility, a critical literacy that leads both students and teachers to interrogate their multiple and complex realities and to see the power of their own language for transformation.

Teachers, too, are taught in ways that reinforce the facade of cultural superiority, and hence we remain oblivious to the ways in which our instructional practices are ideologically situated. Although I had many caring and committed professors, what I learned in most of my courses were ways to teach students how to adapt to the system, rather than ways to accommodate the practices of schooling to meet the needs of students. While attending graduate school in the 1970s and 1980s, I learned new teaching methods, acquired better ways of assessing students' linguistic behaviors, and gained invaluable insights into the reading process itself. I learned about reading strategies, whole language–based teaching, and ways to put phonics in proper perspective. Nevertheless, over the years I always felt that there was something missing in our literacy research and practice, for while we were talking about the best way to teach literacy, students continued to drop out of school in record numbers; teenage suicide and pregnancy rates continued to increase; and violence in the home and on the street began reaching epidemic proportions. What was wrong with the questions we were asking?

It has only been recently, in working with teachers and students from cultures other than my own, that I began to realize that what was missing was our failure to acknowledge that literacy is both a cultural and a social expression, and therefore it is always inherently political. Literacy practices operate within a sociopolitical context, and that context is defined and legitimated by those who have the power and authority to do so. This context shapes our worldview—our perspectives, our notions about how things ought to be—in such a way that the underlying value assumptions often remain latent, becoming embedded in the structures and material forms of schooling. Hence, it is only through conscious reflection and critique, or what critical theorists refer to as *praxis,* that genuine transformation is able to occur. Through my own praxis, I have come to realize that our literacy practices reflect the hegemonic order in that they are based upon the hierarchical power structure that exists within society as a whole—a power structure that determines whose culture gets legitimated, and whose becomes marginalized.

Today, I instruct practitioners who teach in the same system that worked for me and for them but has failed so many others. They, too, are frustrated by the system, a system where there is too much blame and too few rewards, a system where they are controlled, sanctioned, and tremendously overworked, a system that tells them what to teach and how to teach it and then implies that they are responsible for society's failures. In my own practice, my aim is to encourage my students to engage in a critical praxis, so that they too might come to an understanding of the reproductive tendencies of education to perpetuate the status quo, and the transformative potential of education to change it.

This, too, is the aim of this book. In the pages that follow, I examine how the teaching of literacy is both a social and cultural act, and therefore also a moral act—one that involves making decisions about our relationships with others and with our world. This volume embraces a conception of morality that is driven by an obligation to work for the common good, that is motivated by compassion and care for others and for the physical universe, that encompasses a commitment to equity, and that acknowledges the inherent value of all living things. As we come to understand literacy as a moral imperative, then literacy instruction requires that we make choices concerning issues of ownership, equity, and power. My purpose in writing this volume is not to present definitive answers; rather, my intent is to encourage dialogue so that we might begin to acknowledge and interrogate the perspectives we bring to our pedagogical practices. In the pages that follow, I show the ways in which the terms *literacy* and *illiteracy* have become symbolic of particular social and cultural realities. While literacy is commonly thought of in neutral terms, as the ability to read and write, in pragmatic terms literacy is no longer construed so simplistically. To view literacy as a mere tool is to obscure the social—and hence, the political—ramifications of written language use in Western society. In chapter 1, I explore our common conceptualizations of literacy and look at the role of culture in literacy development. I argue that, because both written and oral language have social functions and are developed within particular sociocultural contexts, our notions about literacy and illiteracy therefore become political constructs, reflecting hegemonic relationships that exist in the larger society.

Schools are institutions responsible for socializing students to accept the norms of the dominant culture. In chapter 2, I examine the underlying ideological assumptions of schooled literacy, that is, literacy as it has come to be conceptualized within the educational institution. Three myths are addressed: (1) the notion that the standard discourse is inherently superior to other linguistic forms; (2) the notion that borrowing conventions from science and technology will result in improved instructional practices; and (3) the notion that literacy instruction and research can, and ought to be, neutral. I examine how certain Eurocentric perspectives have become embedded in both educational research and literacy instruction and how, consequently, our pedagogical practices are not neutral, but rather they tend to reflect the interests of those in power.

The effects of schooled literacy for both teachers and students is the subject of the next chapter. The marginalization of the cultural knowledge of nonmainstream groups creates tensions in the lives of students whose language and experiences are inconsistent with the norms of schooling. Hence, schooled literacy contributes to a system of passivity and resistance that has led to widespread educational failure, particularly among nonmainstream students. Further, relationships of care and trust between students and teachers—relationships that are essential for learning to occur—have been systematically eroded through an emphasis upon standardization and the denial of alternative perspectives.

The remaining chapters in this book examine the aims of literacy instruction for a pluralistic democracy and the pedagogical practices that can help to achieve those aims. A commitment to democracy is simultaneously a commitment to freedom of thought and to open dialogue. Thus, the language of schooling ought to be one that welcomes controversy, that invites diverse perspectives and productive critique, and that encourages us to confront our ethnocentric assumptions and biases. A commitment to democracy also requires a dedication to the values that sustain our democratic traditions: freedom, equity, and social justice. Therefore, a society that is driven by democratic values must also be willing to challenge the forces that undermine the realization of those values—forces of oppression, unearned privilege, prejudice, and institutionalized racism that have come to characterize contemporary American life. I argue in chapter 5 that literacy instruction ought to be consciously political, that literacy ought to be taught in ways that illuminate the hegemonic functions of language and knowledge and that nurture a critical social consciousness, so that students and teachers become cognizant of the ways in which they are both victims of and unwitting corroborators in a system of dominance and control.

Finally, literacy ought to be taught in ways that enable students and teachers to understand the transformative potential of language, so that they can challenge the inequitable distribution of power and the culture of acquiescence that sustains it. Transformation, as it is being conceptualized here, is not merely a means for individual liberation; rather, it is a quest for equity, a moral vision that is grounded in an ethic of compassion and care. What is needed, therefore, is a more critical literacy or, in the words of Lankshear and Lawler (1987), a literacy that enables students to become properly literate: a literacy of hope and possibility, of affirmation and acceptance; a literacy that challenges us to look beyond our limited cultural assumptions and worldviews; a literacy that not only legitimates students' voices but allows them to see that they are part of the continuing human dialogue, and that their lives can make a difference. If this book helps us to envision such a literacy, then it will have served its purpose.

# 1

## Conceptualizing Literacy

At the end of one of the longest, most difficult hours of my own life, the students voted, unanimously, to preface their individual messages with a paragraph composed in the language of Reggie Jordan. "At least we don't give up nothing else. At least we stick to the truth: Be who we been. And stay all the way with Reggie."

It was heartbreaking to proceed, from that point. Everyone in the room realized that our decision in favor of Black English had doomed our writings, even as the distinctive reality of our Black lives always has doomed our efforts to "be who we been" in this country.

I went to the blackboard and took down this paragraph dictated by the class:

YOU COPS!
WE THE BROTHER AND SISTER OF WILLIE JORDAN, A FELLOW STONY BROOK STUDENT WHO THE BROTHER OF THE DEAD REGGIE JORDAN. REGGIE, LIKE MANY BROTHER AND SISTER, HE A VICTIM OF BRUTAL RACIST POLICE, OCTOBER 25, 1984. US APPALL, FED UP, BECAUSE THAT ANOTHER SENSELESS DEATH WHAT OCCUR IN OUR COMMUNITY. THIS WHAT WE FEEL, THIS, FROM OUR HEART, FOR WE AIN'T STAYIN' SILENT NO MORE. (June Jordan, "Nobody Mean More to Me Than You and the Future Life of Willie Jordan," 1988, pp. 363–74)

This letter was written by a group of university students shortly after the brutal killing of twenty-five-year-old Reggie Jordan, the brother of a fellow classmate, by two White Brooklyn police officers. It represents the culmination of a study of Black English—a study that engendered a spirit of pride and dignity in their own identity as African Americans, and in the language that symbolizes that identity. These students had come to see the potential of written language to inspire, to empower, to give voice to those who otherwise might not be heard. Thus, when an unarmed Reggie Jordan was killed, point blank, by policemen's bullets and the officers were never prosecuted, and when the New York City Police Department was unable to provide the family with a plausible explanation for the death, these students chose to express their outrage and to assert their humanity through writing. They decided to use the discourse that Reggie Jordan would have used—a discourse that celebrated his identity and that validated his life. Their letter was never published. Jordan (1988, p. 373) writes:

> *Newsday* rejected the piece.
> *The Village Voice* could not find room in their "Letters" section to print the individual messages from the students to the police. None of the TV news reporters picked up the story.
> Nobody raised $180,000 to prosecute the murder of Reggie Jordan.
> *Reggie Jordan is really dead.* (emphasis mine)

What happens when our language is rejected? When our voice is silenced? When we are told, in often subtle ways, that our discourse—our natural, inherent way of communicating—is inferior to the language of others?

The judgments we make about literacy, both as educators and as members of a pluralistic society, are moral ones. They reflect what we consider to be good, right, and virtuous. In our discussions of literacy, we often assume that we know what is morally right. Obviously, in a society that depends upon reading and writing for continued economic advancement, literacy is "right" and illiteracy is "wrong," and hence the moral obligation of schools is to make everyone literate. Indeed, in recent decades the eradication of illiteracy has become a national priority. Literacy has become linked to societal advancement, and schools have been charged to provide so-called equal opportunities so that all might have equal access to society's limited rewards.

Perhaps, however, things are a bit more complicated than this. According to common standards for assessing literacy (which is generally measured by number of years of schooling), the students in June Jordan's class were obviously literate. In fact it could be argued that, because they had spent a great deal of time analyzing the structure of their language and were aware of linguistic differences, they were more advanced in their understanding of written language than most university students. Nevertheless, in many ways their written prose was judged to be illiterate or, at the very least, unworthy of publication. The question that emerges, therefore, is this: How is literacy perceived in the popular mind, and in what ways is this perception being used to empower some, and to silence others?

Literacy has been conceptualized in a variety of ways. Some theorists suggest that literacy is the ability to decode print into speech. Others suggest that literacy is the ability to acquire meaning from written text. Still others regard literacy as the ability to read and write at a specified proficiency level. In this

chapter, I show that how we define literacy is more than just an exercise in se-
mantics. Rather, our perceptions about literacy are based upon certain ideological perspectives, and therefore the way literacy is defined has profound
implications for the ongoing literacy debate.

I would argue that a major problem with current definitions of literacy is
that they tend to ignore the social and cultural dimensions of both spoken and
written language. Perceptions that confine literacy to a technological input-
output model of meaning acquisition distort the nature of communication
and ignore the way language is acquired within sociocultural contexts. As I
show in this chapter, reading and writing, like speaking, are inherently social
and cultural acts. I also claim that, because written language is always constituted within specific contexts, it always carries certain political (and hence,
moral) implications; its use can never be neutral.

## THE SOCIAL AND CULTURAL CONSTRUCTION OF LITERACY

To understand literacy as both a social and a cultural process, it is important
to examine theoretical perspectives concerning language acquisition and use.
Popular notions of reading and writing generally obscure the fact that written language is *language*. By disregarding current wisdom about children's
linguistic development, erroneous conceptions about literacy have emerged
that tend to ignore both the cognitive and social dimensions of written language learning (Edelsky 1991). Language—both oral and written—is a symbolic system, a system of signs used in the process of making meaning. Communication through this symbolic system is functional; that is, it is used for
realizing certain purposes within particular social contexts. In developing language, children learn these functions as they acquire the forms and structures
of language. Hence, learning language is a dynamic, interrelated process. Halliday (1985) suggests that children's language has two essential functions: a
"doing" or pragmatic function that allows children to communicate their desires and intentions ("Let's go out for a walk"), and a "thinking" or mathetic
function that enables them to create meaning and to express their thoughts
("Nice to see you"). In other words, children learn that language is used both
to convey and to explore ideas, and these social functions are acquired and
practiced through participation with others in the act of communicating.

Like spoken language, written language communication is a social process.
Written texts serve different functions from spoken texts, however, in that
they are used to communicate ideas across space and time. Because the environmental context is typically absent in written language, the words must
provide the context for interpretation; hence, written texts tend to have a
more disembedded quality than oral texts (Pappas, Kiefer, and Levstik 1990).
Nevertheless, written texts are still social constructions; authors must con-

sider audience and intent, and readers bring their own interpretations in constructing meaning from the words on the page. Although perhaps not as obvious as the collaboration involved in conversational speech, written language is also collaborative in that it involves a shared participation in the negotiation of meaning.

Both written and spoken texts are created within what Halliday and Hasan (1985) refer to as the "context of situation"—the social environment that determines the register, or form, of the discourse. The context of situation has three components: (1) the field, or what is going on in the course of talking or writing; (2) the tenor, or who is involved in the discourse, including the social status of the participants; and (3) the mode, or what role language is playing in the social event. Consider, for example, the parent-teacher conference as a social and linguistic event. The participants are situated in particular roles and relationships (tenor); they are using oral communication (mode) for the purpose of evaluating the progress of a student (field). These three variables collectively determine the register, that is, the specialized form of the language being used (wording, style of discourse, etc.). In a typical parent-teacher conference, the teacher assumes a more authoritarian role, while the parent(s) assume a more dependent role; the teacher provides information and the parents respond. The discourse (both verbal and nonverbal) is generally more formal in tone, reflecting the nature of the social encounter.

Failure to consider the context of situation in our research and practice can have serious ramifications. For instance, children who perceive the teacher to be representative of the dominant culture, and hence someone who may be critical of their speech patterns, may be noncommunicative in the classroom and therefore may be unable to demonstrate their linguistic competence. Parents who perceive practitioners as experts may feel removed from the school setting; they may therefore be reluctant to communicate with the teacher and to develop an alliance that would be beneficial in educating their child. Form letters sent home as a way of providing information symbolize to some parents the authority of written discourse over oral communication—a value held by those in the educated class—and these hidden messages may have the undesirable effect of alienating those whose social customs favor face-to-face communication. These are just a few examples of how written and oral language have been used by educational institutions in ways that tend to distance their clients, thereby undermining the establishment of positive social relationships. As I argue throughout this book, our tendency to ignore the social dimension of literacy and language use continues to have grievous consequences for both schools and society.

The contexts in which language is learned and used are not only social; they are also cultural. The term *culture* as it is being used here refers to a system of knowledge that allows individuals to interpret events in their lives. *Culture* can be differentiated from a *sociocultural system* that delimits traditions and patterns of life within a community. It is, rather, an ideological system consisting of shared meanings and symbols that have become embedded in daily social encounters. In the words of Keesing (1974, p. 89), culture is "not all of what an individual knows and thinks and feels about his world. It is his theory of what his fellows know, believe, and mean, his theory of the code being followed, the game being played." This theory is used by individuals to interpret events and to govern their behavior.

Because language is a way of making meaning within a given social context, language therefore can be considered a subsystem of culture, that is, a shared symbolic system within the larger cultural system. Hymes (1986) examines language use within various sociolinguistic systems and presents a taxonomy for describing a "speech community," that is, "a community sharing rules for the conduct and interpretation of speech, and rules for the interpretation of at least one linguistic variety" (p. 54). These normative rules for language use become part of a shared system of meaning, or culture. They include expectations for both verbal and nonverbal behaviors, for example, rules for when to talk and how to talk, appropriate topics of conversation, normal durations of silence, interpretations of various statements and other communicative actions, and so on. In other words, the norms governing communication embody "a community's own theory of linguistic repertoire and speech" (Hymes 1986, p. 39; also see Garcia 1994; Gumperz, 1985). Oral and written texts, therefore, not only are linguistically symbolic; they are also culturally symbolic. Particular ways of making meaning are culturally defined, and hence one's language is an integral part of one's identity. In fact, language often becomes our badge of identity, associating us with particular cultural systems. Throughout this book, the school is examined as a type of speech community in that established norms have evolved within the institution that govern linguistic behavior. To be a member of the speech community of the educational institution, therefore, requires that participants share notions about language use on a metacommunicative and largely implicit level, which enables them to convey and interpret messages appropriately.

Studies by Heath (1983) and Taylor and Dorsey-Gaines (1988) show how literacy and language are used to create and share meaning in different sociocultural contexts (i.e., speech communities). Heath documents the development of written and oral language in three different communities in the Piedmont South; Taylor and Dorsey-Gaines examine the uses of literacy in an inner-city community in the Northeast. Both studies document an extensive and diverse use of literacy in the home and community, often despite severe economic hardship. Communication through print in these communities is embedded within daily social encounters and is used for a variety of social functions. Both of these studies document how the familial literacy of the home (as well as the literacy used in other social institutions within the community) differed dramatically from the literacy encountered in school, in that the literacy of the school was essentially disembedded from its social context. Further, familial literacy tends to be a collaborative effort; family members often work together in constructing a shared interpretation of a text. One does not fail familial literacy. School literacy, on the other hand, is typically noncollaborative and is based upon certain standards against which one's literacy behaviors are judged (Varenne and McDermott 1986). In other words, literacy in school reflects the larger society in that it is contrived within a competitive and meritocratic social system that gives some the authority to establish the criteria for evaluation, and hence, the authority to define failure. In fact, schools may be the first institutions in which children encounter this hegemonic function of written language.

Like other sociolinguistic theorists, Gee (1992) suggests that one's use of language, or what he calls "discourse," is essentially an "identity kit." He defines discourse as "a socially accepted association among ways of using language, of thinking, and of acting that can be used to identify oneself as a member of a socially meaningful group or 'social network'" (p. 21). Hence, Gee's notions of a "social network" are similar to Hymes's idea of a "speech community." According to Gee, we each possess a primary discourse that we acquired through socialization within a family unit and cultural group. We acquire other ways of thinking, acting, and using language, however, as we become involved in institutions outside of the family. Gee refers to these discourses as "secondary discourses"—discourses acquired and learned as we interact within secondary institutions such as schools, workplaces, businesses, and so on.

Literacy, according to Gee, involves the control of these secondary discourses. Hence, there are many applications of the term *literacy,* since there are many different secondary discourses. Also, because discourses always involve cultural norms for how one is to speak and act, they are always inherently ideological. For instance, the discourse of management differs from that of workers in that it carries with it certain assumptions and beliefs about how one is to speak and behave in the role of manager. As I argue in the next chapter, the discourse of educational institutions contains ideological assumptions about how one is to speak and behave in the role of student. Thus, in order to be considered literate within corporations, schools, or other institutions, one must master the requisite discourse.

When literacy is viewed in this way, it becomes apparent that there can never be a single definition for literacy; rather, there are shades of literacy and illiteracy within particular social contexts. Thus, some individuals are viewed as being more literate and some as less literate within schools, workplaces, service institutions, and elsewhere, depending upon the norms governing the discourse within that institution. It is also true that each of us is illiterate to a certain degree, in that it is impossible to master all the secondary discourses that are available to us.

It should be further noted, however, that discourses are not given equal status in our society. There are, in fact, what might be called dominant discourses, and there are also discourses that many would consider substandard. Gee (1992) defines dominant discourses as those that can lead to the acquisition of social goods, such as money, power, and status. Groups that have the least conflict in using these discourses are defined as dominant groups. Using this paradigm, it is evident that schools have not traditionally been encouraged to teach all discourses; rather, they have been commissioned to teach a particular discourse, or form of literacy—a literacy that is sanctioned by dominant groups. Accordingly, there is a popular notion that teaching this discourse is basically fair, for each participant is thereby given an equal opportunity to obtain these desirable social goods. What is argued throughout this book, however, is that those who have the power to define literacy are also in the best position to use that definition for advancing their own interests. In other words, their primary discourse is rendered compatible with the dominant discourse. It is further argued that the ways in which literacy is typically taught in schools do not provide the kinds of experiences that allow children to acquire dominant discourses but instead tend to alienate those who already are hindered by an unequal access to power.

## LITERACY AS A NATIONAL PRIORITY

This brings us full circle to our original discussion of literacy as a national priority. Given that we accept the arguments presented thus far that (1) literacy is both socially and culturally constructed, and therefore (2) our conceptions of literacy include ways of speaking and behaving within particular contexts, and not just the ability to produce and understand written texts (i.e., a discourse), how then is literacy being defined in national discussions concerning a literate populace?

I would suggest that a response to this question must involve an examination of the ways in which literacy functions in our society to maintain stability and hence to perpetuate the status quo. It is interesting to consider, for instance, that only one hundred years ago access to literacy was systematically and intentionally denied to a sizeable portion of our population. It was believed that the achievement of even a minimal degree of literacy by persons of color would lead to social and political turmoil. The denial of literacy to subjugated populations, therefore, was used to keep them in their place, so that the hegemonic order might not be disrupted.

Today, it is commonly believed that literacy for all is desirable; in fact, it is deemed essential if our nation is to remain economically competitive in the world market (Shannon 1998). Not only do students need literacy for their own personal development, it has been argued, but clearly "a nation at risk" demands it (Anderson, Hiebert, Scott, and Wilkinson 1985). The literacy that is espoused, however, is generally a functional or basic literacy that allows individuals to function within society as it currently exists. In 1956, W. S. Gray, a prominent reading educator, set the pattern for future definitions of functional literacy. In his UNESCO survey of reading and writing skills, he wrote:

> A person is functionally literate when he has acquired the knowledge and skills in reading and writing which enable him to engage in all those activities in which literacy is normally assumed in his culture or group. (Gray 1956, p. 24; cited in Heap 1988, p. 6)

Consider how this definition of literacy differs from that of Gee. Literacy in a functional sense involves the ability to use only one's primary discourse—to acquire the literacy of one's culture or group. It does not, however, involve the mastery of secondary discourses that would enable individuals to operate outside of their primary group.[1] Therefore, inherent in such definitions is the underlying goal to perpetuate the status quo. Functional literacy maintains social stability in that it allows individuals to be productive citizens and consequently not become drains on the system, while it simultaneously fails to provide them with a true or legitimate literacy in the form of the acquisition of secondary discourses—a literacy that would give them the competence to acquire more authority within the system (and hence, the ability to challenge it).

Assumptions linking literacy and productivity have been applied on a national scale, where it is felt that literacy is directly linked to our ability to remain competitive in an international economic system. While such assumptions may appeal to our common sense, an increasing amount of data shows that the connection between literacy and productivity has been seriously overrated and suggestions that link deficient literacy skills with poor job performance are misleading (Berg 1971; Clifford 1984; Graff 1987; Hull 1993). For instance, in their historical review of studies conducted by the armed services as well as those conducted within the educational sector, Stedman and Kaestle (1987) note that research has generally found only a weak correlation between scores on aptitude tests and on-the-job success. It seems that large percentages of workers with only limited academic skills are able to perform at much higher levels. The authors conclude that "Obviously, severe reading deficiencies would interfere with the ability to acquire and hold many jobs, but above a certain threshold, reading level as measured by standardized tests has little to do with job performance" (p. 39).

Hull's (1993) review of the research on workplace literacy would support this conclusion. In fact, Hull notes that studies have tended to show that the tasks required of blue-collar workers often necessitate mastery of skills and abilities that are rarely acknowledged or even recognized by supervisors, and that workers actually perform at much higher capacities than most work-related literacy tests would suggest. She argues that our assumptions about workplace literacy are based upon a view of literacy as "skills" that can be considered outside of their social context: "The popular discourse of workplace literacy centers on the skills that people lack. . . . such judgments are almost never informed by observations of work, particularly observations that incorporate the understandings of workers" (pp. 33–34).

Additionally, research has demonstrated that an individual's ability to become upwardly mobile has had little to do, historically, with the possession of reading and writing per se; rather, upward mobility has been found to be directly related to one's social and economic position in society. For instance, Harvey Graff (1987) examined literacy in Ontario in the 1860s and 1870s and found little correlation between skilled labor and the possession of literacy. He writes that "large numbers of men, lacking education, assumed positions of skill," whereas "seventy-five per cent of the unskilled and ninety-three per cent of the semi-skilled possessed the skills of literacy" (pp. 168–69). Graff further states that

> illiterate workers were far from a homogeneous lot; indeed, they possessed a social ordering within their own ranks, one which duplicated that of the larger society. As such, Irish Catholics, illiterate or not (though the larger group of illiterates) and the aged (again, most often illiterate) are generally found in the lowest classes, occupational or economic. Much more than mere literacy operated in the establishment and maintenance of the stratification system of the nineteenth century. Education alone would not often dramatically affect class or social status. (p. 171)

In the United States, persons of color have traditionally been denied access to higher-level jobs, despite the acquisition of basic reading and writing skills (McCarthy 1988; Ogbu 1987, 1990). Thus, one's position in the labor force often seems to be much more dependent upon the possession of particular cultural capital than upon the achievement of a certain minimal level of literacy.

If literacy does not automatically lead to enhanced economic development, then we might ask why literacy has come to dominate discussions of societal advancement. Hull (1993) argues that it is common in discussing worker inadequacy to emphasize worker deficits, particularly those often associated with minorities, who historically have been denied access to higher-status jobs.[2] While the problems associated with a lagging economy are, in actuality, complex and multifaceted, there is a certain logic in the current rhetoric: "workers lack literacy, jobs require more literacy, therefore workers are to blame for trouble at work and employers are faced with remedial training" (p. 27).

This thinking tends to be accepted uncritically despite evidence to the contrary. For example, findings presented at the 1989 World Economic Forum suggest that "human resources, including education and training, is only one factor among ten that affect a country's international competitiveness" (p. 30). Nevertheless, blue-collar workers serve as a convenient scapegoat for our diminishing economic rewards. Attributing a failing economy to a seemingly illiterate workforce is, in other words, a classic case of victim blaming and fails to consider other factors that are often more significant, such as the conflicting interests of labor and management, and the deskilling and displacement of workers.

In addition, it could be argued that there are other, more subtle reasons for our current national enthusiasm for literacy. Researchers who have studied the various roles of literacy in both Western and less-developed societies have concluded that basic literacy has traditionally served as a mechanism for control by reinforcing mainstream values. For instance, Street (1984) examines the national literacy campaigns of a number of developing nations and documents how these campaigns primarily have functioned to indoctrinate the rural citizenry with the dominant ideology associated with modernization and nationalization. Likewise, Graff (1987) shows how literacy was used in the early industrial era in England to manage the laboring workforce. He writes that "to 'educate' the workers was the problem. It was not an education in reading and writing, but rather it was the need to train them to a new work discipline, permeated with the middle class obsession with character and morality" (p. 66). Cook-Gumperz (1986) notes that widespread popular literacy in nineteenth-century England actually preceded mass schooling, and "schooling was considered both in Europe and in America as a means of bringing popular literacy under the control of publicly organised school systems" (p. 27). Lankshear and Lawler (1987) trace how the laboring class struggled to overcome this ideological domination by maintaining a countervailing voice.

In the United States, as in England and elsewhere, literacy has played a major role in transmitting the national ideology and socializing students into the mainstream culture, and the responsibility for teaching literacy (and hence, for inculcating dominant values through legitimating the dominant discourse) has largely become the province of schools. Illiteracy, therefore, has become a convenient means for concealing the complex economic and social realities of our times, and, as we examine in the next chapter, its gatekeeping function continues to be ensured through our instructional practices.

Functional or basic literacy, then, has a decidedly political role. By providing individuals with coping skills to get by in society, it actually serves to disempower learners by limiting their access to, and hence their acquisition of, secondary discourses—those discourses that would make them truly literate according to dominant standards. As Lankshear and Lawler write:

> To be functionally literate . . . comprises a minimal, essentially negative, passive state. The functionally literate person can at best cope with their world. They manage to fill in job application forms, having read the advertisement for the job.

They may even get the job and, in that event, survive in it assisted by the ability to read bus and train timetables, job instructions, order forms, and the like. To be functional here is to be not unable to cope with the most minimal routines and procedures of mainstream existence in contemporary society. . . . Functional literacy equips the person to respond to outside demands and standards, to understand and follow. There is no suggestion here of leading, commanding, mastering or controlling. (1987, p. 64)

Functional literacy, in fact, plays a critical role as we move from an industrial to an information age. Consistent with a skills model of written language development, a functionalist model conceptualizes reading and writing as essentially neutral decoding/encoding processes. The possession of reading and writing skills facilitates the transmission of information, yet does not demand critical reflection. The functionalist perspective, therefore, allows individuals to learn the so-called facts of U.S. history without examining the various social and economic struggles that have shaped current policies. It permits the dissection of literary texts (e.g., symbolism, characterization, plot development, etc.) without a critical inquiry into the sociopolitical context that influences the construction and interpretation of those texts. It encourages a cursory reading of popular publications such as newspapers and magazines, without a deeper understanding of the historical developments that have led to contemporary problems. Written language, in this sense, is viewed as a "conduit" (Bowers 1988)—as a means for sending and receiving seemingly neutral information, rather than as a means for promoting critical analysis. As argued in the next chapter, this view of literacy obscures human authorship and consequently denies the social and cultural dimensions of written language.

The tracking and sorting practices that occur in schools tend to reinforce these notions of literacy, in that the acquisition of functional literacy in the form of basic skills is emphasized in the lower tracks (Oakes 1985). Therefore, students in lower achievement groups are rarely accorded the opportunity to use language in ways that would empower them through the acquisition of secondary discourses. Thus, by emphasizing only limited competencies, those students who are the most oppressed are denied access to a form of literacy that would allow them to negotiate out of their subordinate position and enable them to create their own social realities (Freire and Macedo 1987).

## LITERACY AND GOODNESS

To be considered truly literate in our society requires the attainment of a particular manner of speaking and writing as well as the acquisition of a specified body of knowledge. There have, in fact, emerged various shades of literacy and illiteracy in our society, depending upon whose standards are being used. Hence, individuals from a particular speech community whose linguistic behavior is inconsistent with the norms of the dominant community may be considered illiterate, despite the possession of reading and writing skills. In the words of Hull (1993, p. 31), "we are more likely to view as deficient, different, and separate those who are not or do not appear to be conventionally literate."

Perhaps nowhere has the relationship between literacy and the hegemonic order become more apparent than through the popular endorsement of what E. D. Hirsch (1987) has called "cultural literacy," which equates literacy with the acquisition of a particular body of knowledge. Hirsch argues that reading and writing are not processes that are devoid of content but, rather, are dependent upon a shared understanding of American culture. The national culture he advocates, however, does not include the knowledge and traditions of persons of color or other marginalized groups. Rather, what Hirsch seems to be suggesting is that, in order to be considered literate, one must be knowledgeable about "high culture" (Scholes 1986) or, in the words of Erickson (1984), one must be "lettered." This ideology is further reflected in the emphasis upon a common curriculum and standard language, both of which are designed to promote national unity and cultural integration.

Because written and oral texts are socially and culturally constructed, they represent particular realities—the realities of those who have the authority to define them at any given moment in any given social and linguistic event. As Knoblauch and Brannon (1993) suggest, words become symbols of representation, ways of "naming the world." In groups shaped by a shared culture and mutual goals, individuals collaborate in defining their realities, in naming their worlds. Within the larger community, however, the power to name resides with that elusive *other*—with those who have the authority to construct a reality that counts, with those who have been accorded the ultimate authority to know.

In his provocative book entitled *The Moral and Spiritual Crisis in Education*, David Purpel (1989) argues that popular rhetoric tends to suggest a moral conviction of equality. We celebrate the founding doctrines of our democratic nation that state that all are created equal, that all are born with certain inalienable rights. This rhetoric is based upon the fundamental notion of human dignity—the idea that all men and women, regardless of class or race, have inherent worth. At the same time, however, social reality defies equity by demanding that we prove our value through achievement. That is, in our hegemonic system, persons are not automatically deemed to be okay; rather, we must earn our right to dignity and respect through our achievements. Thus, while "our democratic principles involve a rejection of the notion of ascribed hierarchy . . . as a people we congratulate ourselves not for rejecting privilege but only for redefining the conditions under which people may have privileges" (p. 35).

The perpetuation of social privilege requires the establishment of criteria for measuring an individual's worth, and a crucial standard for evaluating merit is our use of oral and written language. Hence, both the actual possession of reading and writing and the ways in which language is used translate into a privileged entitlement to certain cultural commodities. What becomes even more problematic, however, is that it is the perception of the possession of literacy—determined by norms associated with the dominant discourse—that is used to calculate one's status.

Within such a world, terms such as *literacy* and *illiteracy* become symbols of representation: *illiterate* connotes ignorance, indolence, and a general lack of goodness, while *literate* conveys knowledge, ambition, and high ethical standards. The illiterate are creating economic havoc; the literate must retrieve the resulting losses and, at the same time, convince the illiterate to become more like them. Hence *literate* and *illiterate* no longer are used solely to identify one's state of literacy; rather, these terms are used to identify those who are more deserving or less deserving of society's limited rewards. In other words, in our contemporary society, literacy functions not only as a means for transmitting information. It also functions as a means for separating the more worthy from the less worthy, thereby justifying a system of meritocracy whereby those who have the highest literacy achievement—as measured against the dominant discourse—are awarded the most goods.

Our views of language have not been conceived in a vacuum. Not only have our perceptions of literacy and illiteracy been shaped within a hegemonic system, but we exist in a society that values objectivity and rational decision making over subjective ways of knowing. Since written language facilitates the transmission and manipulation of knowledge, literacy has come to assume a prominent position in our rational system. Knoblauch and Brannon (1993) write:

> There can be no question . . . that literacy is truly necessary to survival and success in the contemporary world—a world that enjoys its authority to set the terms of survival and success, a world that reading and writing abilities have significantly shaped in the first place. But it's important to regard that necessity in the context of ideological conditions that have accounted for it, or else we sacrifice the humanizing, not to say humbling, understanding that life can be otherwise than the way we happen to know it—and that people who are measured positively by the yardstick of literacy enjoy their privileges in life because of their power to choose and apply that instrument on their own behalf, not because of their intelligence, point of "development," or other innate worthiness. (p. 16)

As we examine in the next chapter, technical, scientific models of written and oral language use have obtained prominence, whereby language is used to transmit seemingly neutral information. As the goal of schooling increasingly has become one of acquiring and processing greater amounts of information, such rationalized models have come to characterize school literacy.

Yet many have also begun to acknowledge that, in our emphasis upon objective reasoning, we have ignored important subjective dimensions of our existence—those aesthetic, emotional, and spiritual qualities that shape our ethical character and that connect us to others at a metaphysical level. The dominant discourse, however, tends to marginalize these ways of knowing, promoting literacy standards that amplify objective knowledge and that value the acquisition and transmission of empirical data. It is indeed difficult for those of us who have been socialized to accept the superiority of a highly rational and literate world to envision life differently. Yet it would seem that to deny the importance of other ways of knowing is an exercise in intellectual arrogance; there are, and have been, other perspectives, other important and valid ways of seeing the world.

Thus, I would argue that using dominant notions of literacy as a means for evaluating an individual's intelligence and worth is an inherently moral decision. It is a decision, conditioned by the rationality of modernity, that values certain ways of knowing over others. It is also a decision that is largely implicit, having been formed within a system of stratification that rewards behaviors associated with the dominant discourse—behaviors that have been designated as desirable by those who have the authority to constitute them; behaviors that are typically associated with being White, upper-class, and male. As discussed in the next chapter, the dominant ideology becomes obscured in our instructional practices; it becomes, in a sense, a part of the very fabric of schooling. Hence, most educators are blind to the moral implications of their actions, for they are products of the same pedagogy that conceals the political dimension of literacy and schooling for most of our students.

I would suggest that what is needed in our society is a different definition of literacy—one that acknowledges the hegemonic power structure and that values the discourses of groups that traditionally have been marginalized. Such a literacy would enable students to question and to engage in critical dialogue so that they might be educated for participation in a democracy. It would provide a means for identifying and reflecting upon those ideological and social conditions that serve to profit a few at the expense of many. Literacy, in this sense, would become truly functional in that it would enable individuals to critique their individual and collective histories and to begin to see themselves as part of an ongoing narrative of experience (McLaren and Giroux 1997).

Beyond this, however, a reconstituted definition of literacy would enhance our capacity for altruism. Our troubled world cries out for justice, equity, and human understanding. Yet dominant views of literacy tend to diminish our subjective selves, inhibiting our ability to acquire a critical social consciousness. Literacy as a moral imperative envisions language as functioning in a transformative way—as a means for seeing the world differently—so that we might begin to construct a more humane and compassionate society. Hence, we must move beyond narrow, limiting conceptions of literacy toward a recognition of its transformative potential; we must embrace a literacy that will illuminate reality so that we might ultimately be able to reinvent that reality. To do so requires an examination of the ideological assumptions that frame literacy as it is currently being conceptualized in schools, a topic addressed in the next chapter.

## NOTES

1.  An alternate interpretation is also possible here. Gray's reference to one's "culture or group" may also imply a single or unitary national culture, which denies the reality of cultural pluralism and the hegemonic function of language. As I have already argued, such interpretations ignore the social and cultural dimensions of written language.

2.  I acknowledge that the very use of the term *minority* implies marginalization and, in fact, is an erroneous concept in our increasingly pluralistic society. Nevertheless, it is also erroneous to categorize all castelike groups as "persons of color" since, as I argue elsewhere (Eller 1989a), certain subcultural groups of European descent also have been exploited for economic gain and coerced into accepting mainstream standards. Hence, the term *minority* here is used generically and applies to groups who historically have remained outside the dominant culture.

# 2

# Schooled Literacy as an Ideological Construct

Class and culture erect boundaries that hinder our vision—blind us to the logic of error and the everpresent stirring of language—and encourage the designation of otherness, difference, deficiency. And the longer I stay in education, the clearer it becomes to me that some of our basic orientations toward the teaching and testing of literacy contribute to our inability to see. (Mike Rose, *Lives on the Boundary*, 1989, p. 205)

Within the academy there has emerged a special kind of language that we as educators use to talk about literacy—a language that confirms our professionalism, that shows we are members of an elite literacy club, that gives us the authority to define failure. Academic discourse is powerful; it simultaneously privileges and marginalizes. Knowing this language implies that we have something important to say; not knowing it reveals ignorance, and with it, the right for those who know to dismiss alternate voices, to categorize, to blame the victim.

In his moving account of his own life as an educator, Mike Rose (1989) describes the ways in which prevailing views about literacy have been tainted by the dominant discourse. Having witnessed the struggles of Mexican Americans, Vietnam veterans, and underprepared freshman at UCLA, Rose examines how traditional schooling has worked to disenfranchise members of the intellectual underclass by defining them as deficient, disabled, in need of remediation. The language of the academy promotes separateness; individuals are seen as culturally deprived, linguistically disadvantaged, lacking the motivation to succeed. Further, the prose of academe creates a form of linguistic exclusion that denies educational parity for those who need it the most.

In an effort to assure that all students have an equal opportunity for success, schools purport to endorse a pedagogy that is essentially value free. Researchers, too, make a conscious effort to overcome their own subjectivity, and the validity of literacy studies is determined largely by adherence to the basic tenets of scientific empiricism in both the research design and the interpretation of results. Hence, it is generally assumed that schools are nonpolitical sites in which all belief systems are given legitimacy, and that best practice has been determined through objective inquiry.

Yet the words that we use to frame, to describe, to categorize, are symbolic of the ideological assumptions from which they emerge. They reflect a dominant perspective—a particular worldview—that guides our expectations and interpretations, that defines how the world is supposed to be. Hence, those of us who have succeeded are commended for our intelligence and insight; those whose lives lie outside the mainstream are seen as different, in need of the assistance of those who know.

In literacy research and instruction, such rationalities often become obscured in a variety of debates: direct versus indirect instruction, quantitative versus qualitative research, phonics versus whole language, and so on. The arguments that fuel these debates are based upon what generally is considered to be unbiased research—carefully developed research questions and procedures that have elicited tangible outcomes. While the issues themselves may be important, in all of these debates the underlying assumptions that guide our discussions—indeed, that shape the very language we use—often remain implicit.

Literacy is socially constructed; in the process of becoming literate, individuals acquire the norms governing literate behavior within specific social contexts. Because literacy is socially and culturally defined, it carries political implications. That is, literacy is inherently ideological in that it is "always qualified by the context of assumptions, beliefs, values, expectations, and related conceptual material that accompanies its use by particular groups of people in particular sociohistorical circumstances" (Knoblauch and Brannon 1993, p. 15). Thus, the ways in which written language is taught always reflect a particular ideology about what constitutes appropriate literate behavior. By focusing solely on pedagogical and procedural issues, the political nature of literacy becomes obscured.

In this chapter, I examine several underlying assumptions about literacy as it is frequently defined within the school context. Like other theorists (Collins 1989; Cook-Gumperz 1986), I am choosing to use the term *schooled literacy* to characterize the type of literacy promoted by our educational institutions. Schooled literacy is conceptualized here as a discourse that carries with it certain expectations for thinking, behaving, and using language (both oral and written). Because it is generally acquired outside one's primary social network, it is therefore a secondary discourse, consisting of a number of subdiscourses (depending upon the situational context), and it is used for gauging success or failure within the institution. In this chapter, I attempt to illuminate the beliefs associated with this discourse and to show how these beliefs become operationalized through our pedagogical practices. By making these value assumptions explicit, I hope to develop a greater appreciation for how our unspoken notions about literacy affect the ways in which we view and interpret important issues in the field, and, in fact, even determine what issues we consider to be important.

## UNDERLYING VALUE ASSUMPTIONS
## OF SCHOOLED LITERACY

In the remainder of this chapter, the following three implicit assumptions of schooled literacy are explored.

(1) There are certain discourses that are more literate than other discourses, and therefore are inherently superior;
(2) Borrowing conventions from science and technology will result in superior instructional programs and practices;
(3) Literacy instruction and research can—and ought to be—neutral.

### Assumption No. 1

The first assumption underlying schooled literacy is that certain discourses are more literate than other discourses, and therefore they are inherently superior. As noted in chapter 1, written and oral languages always involve communicating to realize certain intentions: to be entertained, to express one's views, to obtain information. These intentions are constructed within particular social and cultural contexts. Consider, for example, the oral and written texts found in various religious services, or the sub rosa uses of literacy in schools (e.g., note passing and graffiti). These texts all have distinct and predictable patterns and styles of discourse, or particular registers, based upon the context of the situation in which they are used.

Because literacy is socially constructed, it is erroneous to conceive of literacy as a single, unified entity; rather, we must begin to recognize that there are many different literacies, depending upon the context within which it is being construed. What is considered appropriate literate behavior in one context may be unacceptable in another context (de Castell, Luke, and MacLennan 1986; Gilmore 1987, 1992; Heath 1983; Shuman 1986). In the words of Lankshear and Lawler, "what literacy *is* is entirely a matter of how reading and writing are conceived and practised within particular social settings" (1987, p. 43). The classroom represents a specific social setting and has its own criteria that govern the appropriateness of oral and written texts. In other words, school is a social institution, and therefore it has developed characteristic discourses, with accompanying norms that govern our ways of thinking, acting, and using language.

As discussed in the previous chapter, discourses carry with them certain values, beliefs, and attitudes that are mastered through access to the social practices accompanying language use. Research has shown that all linguistic systems are equally complex and that all ways of communicating and receiving meaning are valuable (Houston 1970; Labov 1985). Nevertheless, there continues to be an implicit assumption, reminiscent of verbal deficit theories popularized in the 1960s, that nonstandard linguistic forms are deficient and that speakers of variant dialects are verbally deprived (Eller 1989b; Horvath 1977). Sociolinguists have long recognized that language use reflects social relationships; hence, the discourses of those who traditionally have been marginalized—those who are seen as being less worthy of society's rewards—can never become the "discourses of power" (Perry and Delpit 1998).

Schools, therefore, are charged with the task of teaching certain forms of language use, or discourses, forms that are based upon dominant standards and behaviors. The discourses valued by schools are, in the words of James Paul Gee, dominant or "middle-class mainstream" sorts of discourses—discourses that tend to embrace linguistic norms that are consistent with those of the ruling class (1989, 1992). Since all students must become proficient in using dominant discourses, schooling would appear to promote equity for all. Yet the fact remains that the primary discourses of some (White, middle- or upper-class) students better prepare them for the linguistic demands of school than the primary discourses of other (non-White, lower-class) students. (Consider, for example, those students whose parents are well educated, and consequently are considered highly literate according to society's standards.)

Christie (1987) argues that, in English-speaking societies, written language has gained precedence over spoken language, and therefore we tend to apply "written-language-like" criteria to oral discourse. She writes:

> How many of us . . . have heard some passage of talk condemned as "ungrammatical" or "poorly expressed," when all that is involved is that the text is speech, not written language? The fact is that the grammatical rules invoked to make such judgments apply to written language on the whole, and not to speech at all. (p. 27)

Hence, the primary oral discourses of some children, Christie suggests, do not always provide the requisites necessary for producing certain school "genres"—those schematic structures of experience that are valued by our educational institutions. In other words, students' primary discourses may be incompatible with those required within the school setting, where language use is typically more decontextualized (Cazden 1988).

Those students whose primary discourses tend to be inconsistent with those of the dominant culture generally find themselves at a disadvantage in school in other ways as well. A number of investigations have shown that teachers are inclined to have lower expectations for students whose attitudes, behaviors, and linguistic styles do not conform to the norms of schooled literacy (Collins and Michaels 1986; Gilmore 1987, 1992; Goldenberg 1989; Ortiz 1988; Rist 1970). Often, such expectations operate at an unconscious level, representing implicit criteria shaped within a hegemonic system. Students who are more like the teacher—who share cultural expectations for communication—are regarded as possessing the requisite qualities for school success. Those students who lack this "reciprocity of perspective" (Keddie 1971), however, often find themselves outside of the intellectual arena, unable to verbalize their accumulated knowledge or to demonstrate their linguistic competence.

In a fifteen-year longitudinal study, Gordon Wells (1986) examined patterns of language use found in the home and in school. He found that in the home, children typically engaged in conversation about as much as adults. In school, however, there was a significant imbalance in favor of teacher-talk, and therefore there were substantially fewer opportunities for students to engage in meaningful communication. Furthermore, differences in linguistic ability that are often thought to be related to social class were unsubstantiated. Differences were found, however, in the quality of teacher-student interactions, and these differences were related to teachers' perceptions of linguistic competence. Wells reports that

> there are class-related differences in [children's] ability to cope with tests and testlike situations, and the teachers of the children in our study certainly perceived their oral language abilities to differ in ways that were quite strongly related to family background. . . . Where there were high expectations, teachers were more likely to encourage children to express their ideas spontaneously and to do so at length; conversely, low expectations led to a more strongly eliciting style of conversation on the part of the teacher, with few opportunities for the child to initiate or sustain a topic of conversation. . . . The result is that, with different opportunities, children produce different performances, which merely serve to confirm the teachers' initial expectations. (p. 143)

Wells's research shows how teacher expectation can be a determining factor in a child's linguistic development within the educational institution. Yet, as other studies have also revealed, perceptions of linguistic deficiency resulting from lower-class status are essentially erroneous. A rigid sorting system merely reinforces and legitimizes what might otherwise remain more opaque: children who demonstrate mainstream linguistic behaviors generally can be found in the upper academic tracks, whereas those whose linguistic behaviors do not conform to dominant norms are often found in the lower academic tracks (Bennett 1991; Gelb and Mizokawa 1986; Grant and Rothenberg 1986; Oakes 1985; Ogbu 1990).

To succeed in school and to gain entrance into the dominant culture, therefore, students must acquire the dominant discourses; that is, they must be able to use written and spoken language in certain predefined ways (Collins and Michaels 1986; Erickson 1984; Gee 1992; Gilmore 1987, 1992; Shuman 1986; Taylor and Dorsey-Gaines 1988).[1] A large number of students, however, enter school with a primary discourse that is in many ways incompatible with those of the educational establishment, and they must, therefore, be assisted in learning these discourses through meaningful inquiry and collaboration. The acquisition of secondary discourses, and hence the development of literacy, requires that students be allowed to explore various ways of making meaning, to test new understandings, and to examine the social and cultural dimensions of literacy and language use (Delpit 1998).

In other words, students must learn how language works. In order to develop this metalinguistic awareness, students must be invited to investigate linguistic difference and to critique various discourses, including the dominant discourses. They must be encouraged to explore the functional nature of linguistic variation (i.e., register) as it evolves within various social situations. Finally, they must be immersed in authentic uses of language so that they might acquire the extensive linguistic repertoire that is required for communicating their intentions in diverse contexts.[2] (More is said about these instructional strategies in chapter 5.)

In teaching other discourses, however, our instructional practices often emphasize the superficial properties of language, the details of mechanics and correctness, thereby ignoring the importance of social interaction in language acquisition. Gee believes that these properties are emphasized

> precisely because such superficial features are the best test as to whether one was apprenticed in the "right" place, at the "right" time, with the "right" people. Such superficial features are exactly the parts of Discourses most impervious to overt instruction and are only fully mastered when everything else in the Discourse is mastered. Since these Discourses are used as "gates" to ensure that the "right" people get to the "right" places in our society, such superficial features are ideal. (1989, p. 11)

Rather than providing a pedagogy of immersion and critique, literacy instruction in our schools is generally reduced to the mastery of facts, grammatical rules, and basic skills. Thus, schooled literacy reinforces a particular form of language that can be used to differentiate those students that have been "apprenticed" into the "culture of power" (Delpit 1988), while simultaneously denying others the kinds of authentic language experiences that would give them the opportunity to negotiate out of their inferior position.

As a result of these practices, many students may implicitly feel that they will never be able to achieve full literacy according to society's standards, and they may, therefore, put forth minimal effort. In addition, because dominant discourses carry higher status in our society, embracing a dominant discourse often means rejecting the linguistic behaviors associated with one's primary cultural group (and thus, rejecting a part of one's identity). This situation can further disadvantage nonmainstream students, who are often forced to choose between the norms of the dominant culture and those of their community. Hence, as I discuss in the next chapter, an endorsement of particular linguistic standards and the accompanying marginalization of other discourses may cause some students to resist schooled literacy and the values associated with schooling (Erickson 1987; MacLeod 1987/1995; Ogbu 1987, 1990; Reyhner 1992; Solomon 1988; Willis 1977).

It is clear that schooled literacy has gone beyond the ability to use reading and writing merely to function in society. Schooled literacy has, in fact, legitimated certain ways of producing and taking from text, while marginalizing others. At the same time, it has emphasized superficial features of language, thereby denying access to the linguistic experiences that would enable the acquisition of secondary discourses. What has emerged are various shades of literacy and illiteracy, which has led to divisiveness within the school as well as within the larger society (Goody and Watt 1985). Thus, schooled literacy has become a means for categorizing students into the more literate and less literate, sorting students for their future societal roles. By giving precedence to certain discourses and marginalizing those of nonmainstream groups, schools are able to perpetuate the status quo while maintaining the semblance of equality. Such a system, however, ignores the reality of social privilege. As I argue, schooled literacy has also developed certain characteristics that have effectively obscured the political nature of literacy instruction and research.

## Assumption No. 2

The second assumption underlying schooled literacy is that borrowing conventions from science and technology will result in superior instructional programs and practices. Within the popular rhetoric, there is a frequently articulated belief in the supremacy of science and technology for improving our nation's schools. In a recent article, Maurice Holt (1993) states that "if one had to name the single biggest influence on American education during this century, a strong candidate would be not John Dewey but Frederick Winslow Taylor, the father of 'scientific management'" (p. 382). The ability to acquire skills and content ("input") and to measure competency levels ("output") has become pervasive in educational thought, as has the notion of scientific objectivity in educational research. As a result, measurable behavioral objectives have become essential in planning for instruction, and test scores and performance standards have tended to drive curriculum decisions. Further, the skills and content of instruction have been largely determined by individuals who are removed from daily personal encounters with students, and pedagogical practices have become progressively rationalized as a result of a belief in the infallibility of scientific reasoning.

Such notions of objectivism have a long tradition in Western philosophical thought. Dualistic rationalism emerges from the Cartesian principle conceived by Rene Descartes, *cognito, ergo sum* (I think, therefore I am), whereby man is seen as a "sovereign subject . . . an independent consciousness acting upon the sensory Other that surrounds it, heroically subordinating the material world to rational control" (Knoblauch and Brannon 1993, p. 84). Locke advanced the scientific epistemology with his notion of *tabula rasa*—the mind as blank slate, waiting to be filled with empirical data that can be categorized into and consumed by a rational discourse.

Palmer (1983/1993) suggests that schools tend to promote such objective ways of knowing by portraying "the self as *knower*, the world as *known* . . . giving the knowing self supremacy over the known world" (p. 21). This quest for objectivity has separated the knower from the known—a trend, Palmer argues, that can have dangerous repercussions; for when we as knowers become alienated from the world around us, we feel free to act upon it in potentially destructive ways.[3] Further, this mechanistic way of viewing the world has "served to despiritualize and dehumanize, as it focused attention on concerns other than the sanctity of humanity" (Kincheloe 1993, p. 3).

Although modern philosophers generally recognize the limitations of the Cartesian tradition, objectivism has been "*institutionalized* in our habits of thought, our ideals, and our organization of life" (Gelwick 1977, quoted in Palmer 1983/1993, p. 29). Rationality has been deified, and scientific objectivism has become "a compelling force in contemporary life, a force that promotes images of social progress, of evolutionary advancement toward absolute knowledge and control of the physical world" (Knoblauch and Brannon 1993, p. 85). Because such positivistic reasoning has resulted in immense technological advancement in our society and the accompanying economic supremacy of the Western world, objective ways of knowing have achieved dominance, while other, more subjective or common-sense ways of knowing, are discounted. The logic, it seems, is that if technological rationalization and scientific objectivism have led to international superiority, then surely the integration of technology and scientism in the schools will result in an exemplary educational system.

Schools promote objectivism by presenting information as unbiased facts and by removing that which is known from its social and cultural context. Within this epistemological framework, language becomes a tool—a conduit for the transmission and processing of seemingly neutral information—and literacy learning consists of acquiring the skills for using this tool efficiently. Even students become objects, an idea explored more closely in the next chapter. That is, they become parts on the educational assembly line that can be molded into products for our advanced capitalistic society.

In his book *The Struggle to Continue* (1990), Patrick Shannon documents how scientific approaches to literacy instruction historically have taken precedence over more child-centered or community-based approaches. This technocratic rationality still dominates curriculum theory (Apple 1982, 1983) and is manifested in many of our literacy instructional programs and practices, from basal readers to computer software packages and skills management systems (de Castell and Luke 1986; Edelsky 1991; Luke 1988; Shannon 1989, 1992). These programs, and the tests that accompany them, generally promote ritualized, mechanical responses and therefore tend to inhibit creative reasoning and critical debate. The goal becomes the mastery of decontextualized, artificial tasks—tasks that often are based upon erroneous theories about written language (Edelsky 1991). As a result, patterns of thought are established that help shape and maintain relations of power both inside and outside the classroom.

Consider, for example, the use of computer-assisted instruction—a technological advancement that has the potential, according to some, to revolutionize the so-called teaching industry. Software programs designed to promote literacy development generally require students to respond in a linear fashion by supplying the "correct" information. Not only does this type of exercise prohibit divergent thought, but it implies that knowledge is something that is transmitted rather than dynamically constructed—and continually reconstructed—through collaborative discourse (Bowers 1988; Harrington 1993). Further, such programs reduce knowledge to the acquisition of information and establish codes of behavior for both teachers and learners.

Many print materials used in literacy instruction also endorse a scientific, linear view of knowledge. Basal reading programs, for instance, generally consist of a graded anthology of reading selections, as well as practice exercises, management testing systems, and skills "scope and sequence" charts (Anderson, Hiebert, Scott, and Wilkinson 1985). These programs, along with textbooks and other skills management systems, tend to reduce learning to mastering a set of prespecified objectives (Apple 1982, 1983). Knowledge is determined and legitimated by experts outside of the classroom, and the teacher assumes the role of managing the transmission of that knowledge. Such curriculum programs illustrate how power relations are embedded in the material forms of schooling. By denying the importance of legitimate human enquiry, such programs obscure the social, cultural, and political dimensions of literacy and learning.

The negative implications of computer technology and scientific management in education are just beginning to be examined. In his critique of the transmission model and the preeminence of educational computing, C. A. Bowers (1988) warns that there is a danger in confusing *information* with *ideas*. Quoting Roszak (1986), he writes that "information does not create ideas; by itself, it does not validate or invalidate them" (p. 60). With an emphasis upon information and objective data, computers amplify what Bowers calls a "digital" form of thinking, in which discrete bits of information are separated from the whole. The problem with digital thinking is that information is taken out of its social and cultural context, thereby diminishing critical reflection and ignoring the "tacit dimensions of experience, which are a source of meaning, understanding, and pattern" (p. 63). Bowers argues that textbooks, too, have a "primitive, noninteractive language code" (p. 67). Such texts tend to decontextualize human experience and therefore limit the potential for collective agency in a complex and troubled world.

A belief in the infallibility of science is perhaps most evident in prevailing views about educational failure. An emphasis upon scientific, objective ways of knowing has led to the prevalence of a medical model approach to dealing with literacy problems. Students who lag behind in their written language development are often thought to be in need of a thorough diagnosis, followed by an appropriate treatment. Consider the terms used to define their conditions: attention deficit *disorder,* learning *disability,* mentally *impaired, remedial.* The medical discourse implies that such children need to be fixed, and that special programs can be created that will help to remove their deficiencies. What often occurs is that these children are passed from one supposed expert to another in an attempt to discover the hidden cause of their failure—a practice that can result in low self-esteem and a general disenchantment with literacy and schooling (Rose 1989; Taylor 1991).

## Assumption No. 3

The third assumption of schooled literacy is that literacy instruction and research can be—and ought to be—neutral. Emerging within this scientific tradition are popular notions about literacy that suggest that reading and writing are skills that are used to acquire and transmit information. In other words, literacy is a tool that can be used to realize certain cognitive (and hence, economic) goals. Our obsession with literacy as a means for attaining national economic security and international supremacy is based upon this assumption. So too is the belief that literacy research can be conducted in such a way that it is devoid of political implications. The assumption is that reading and writing are *processes* that can be removed from their actual *functions.*

Such notions, however, ignore the fact that literacy is both social and cultural; it is a process that is always used to realize certain intentions within a particular context. To quote Freire: "Literacy and education in general are cultural expressions. You cannot conduct literacy work outside the world of culture because education in itself is a dimension of culture" (Freire and Macedo 1987, p. 53). Thus, while literacy may be considered to be simply a tool or skill, its uses are culturally determined and therefore involve promoting certain values and beliefs and excluding others (Street 1995).

As discussed in the previous chapter, the cultural dimension of literacy is generally ignored by those who have the authority to control the production of knowledge, and, hence, the authority to establish what counts as truth and fact (Apple 1993b; LeCompte and deMarrais 1992). "Knowledge," suggests Fiske, "is never neutral" (1989, p. 149); it is always based upon someone's perception of reality. Conceiving of literacy as an independent process ignores the political agenda of education; schooling in general, and literacy instruction in particular, are forms of acculturation designed to teach dominant perspectives and beliefs—reality as defined by those in power.

Because the dominant reality is so pervasive in Western society, however, it remains largely unexamined, and consequently it is rarely seen as problematic. It has become part of the ontological rhetoric, the collective wisdom that embodies our theories of the world. Yet teachers and researchers are continually making consequential decisions based upon their own ethnocentric perspectives. For instance, what topics are to be studied, and whose interests do they serve? What texts are to be used for instruction, and what values are conveyed through these texts? (Banks [1991], for instance, points out that even seemingly "neutral" concepts such as the "Westward Movement" have different implications when examined from a Native American versus a European American perspective.) What ideological assumptions frame our research questions and the ways in which we obtain our data? As discussed above, even the decision to promote the Standard English vernacular is, in itself, a value judgment. Yet these decisions are rarely seen as political, and therefore they are seldom challenged.

A number of educational theorists have examined how hegemonic relations of power and domination are embedded in the material forms and structures of schooling. In literacy instruction, for example, one way that hegemony is maintained is through our definitions of knowledge and the ways in which that knowledge is transmitted to students. Emerging within a positivist framework, typical literacy practices tend to define knowledge as "information" and "skills" that are predetermined by "experts" in various fields of inquiry. This concept of knowledge is based upon what Freire (1970/1993) has called the "banking" model and others have called the "transmission" model of education (e.g., Cummins 1986; J. Miller 1993), that is, the idea that teaching consists of providing information to students in order to "fill their minds."[4] Schooled literacy, with its emphasis upon the mastery of "essential" skills and facts, is an example of how the banking concept is applied in instructional practice.

The transmission or banking model assumes that knowledge is something that is static, predetermined, and externally defined, rather than something that is culturally and historically constructed and amenable to change through negotiation. It also assumes that knowledge can be atomized, that is, it can be reduced into smaller units that can be transferred more readily (Miller 1993).

Knowledge, then, becomes a possession or commodity, an end in itself; it is not "a means of interpretation or a basis for the initiation of new patterns or ideas or thoughts . . . a question in search of an answer . . . an integral, invigorating aspect of the person as he attempts to make sense of the world" (Kane 1993, p. 112). Rather, it becomes a set of facts that one must master to be considered educated, or, in the case of literacy, a series of skills that one must acquire to become literate according to criteria determined by the educational establishment.

Power, then, is exercised through the transmission of reified knowledge, that is, knowledge that has been systematized and atomized for ease of transference, and learning is seen as an essentially passive process whereby learners acquire knowledge from those who know. Popkewitz (1987) writes: "The banking concept posits knowledge as external to individuals and controlled by those who have power to define and categorize social reality. The social interactions reinforce that notion of power by suggesting that failure to learn is a personal, not institutional, failure" (p. 4). Knowledge represents terrains of power, and the transmission of knowledge and skills becomes a matter of effective management rather than an invitation for collaborative inquiry.

A primary medium for the transmission of reified knowledge is the textbook. It is important to recognize that texts are products of the interests that inform them; textbooks signify what knowledge and whose knowledge gets transmitted, reinforced, and legitimized. The typical textbook used in classrooms tends to mitigate and even omit potentially controversial content—content that might challenge the status quo (Anyon 1983; Apple 1993b; Cherryholmes 1988; Spring 1991). Consequently, the histories and perspectives of nonmainstream groups—those groups who continue to have less power in our stratified society—are generally ignored. Such narratives, when provided at all, are often allocated to an alternative, elective curricula, such as African American history, women's studies, and the like.

Apple (1993a) argues that textbook publishing is a highly competitive enterprise, and therefore textbook content is in large part determined and controlled by national and international markets. Hence, political and ideological controversies in certain key states such as Texas, Florida, and California have had a significant impact upon what counts as legitimate knowledge. He writes:

> The controversies over the form and content of the textbook have not diminished. In fact, they have become even more heated, particularly in the United States. The changing ideological climate has had a major impact on debates over what should be taught in schools and on how it should be taught and evaluated. There is considerable pressure to raise the standards of texts, make them more "difficult," standardize their content, make certain that they place more stress on "American" themes of patriotism, free enterprise, and the "Western tradition," and link their content to statewide and national tests of educational achievement. (p. 201)

Recently, there has been a renewed interest in returning to the sacred traditions of academe, exemplified through the literary canon, which tends to promote Western, Eurocentric perspectives (Bloom 1987; Hirsch 1987). In the words of McLaren (1988, p. 222), the canon represents "a sacred pool of cultural information . . . the mastery of which will usher the student into the forum of national literacy." Inherent in such views is the belief that a return to an elusive Great Tradition will rid us of the cultural erosion that has been responsible for recent societal decay. Literacy, in this view, is seen as a conduit for transmitting high culture, with the assumption that exposure to the cultural heritage of the elite will cause students to embrace traditional values of moral conduct and civic responsibility.

Written texts, therefore, represent controversial terrains. On one side of the debate are those who would advocate a common cultural discourse, one based upon the shared tenets of Western civilization and monolithic notions of received knowledge. On the other side of the debate are those who sound the call for cultural inclusion and for the construction of a pluralistic, participatory democracy. This debate is decidedly political, based upon issues of power. Ultimately, the victors are those who have the authority to define official knowledge, and therefore the power to determine whose voices are represented in school texts and whose are marginalized.[5]

Operating under a premise of neutrality, however, gives us "a moral and political 'holiday,'" leaving us "free to continue teaching under a comforting delusion, oblivious to the actual outcomes of our labours" (Lankshear and Lawler 1987, p. 50). Conceptualizing literacy as a mere tool allows us to design lessons that teach and test the skills of written language without having to examine the implicit assumptions of our actions, or the tacit values that are embedded in the texts we use. It also allows us to be indifferent to the needs of many of our students, who are required to remain in the margins and to digest a form of literacy that devalues their own primary discourse, yet often fails to provide them with the linguistic knowledge that would lead to empowerment.

Such views about the nature of literacy and learning are so deeply ingrained in the material forms and traditions of schooling that they are rarely seen as problematic. Thus teachers, who are themselves products of the academy and who have been strongly influenced by the rhetoric of scientific management (which frequently masquerades as "teacher professionalism"), often fail to engage in a critical praxis that would enable them to illuminate their implicit assumptions about literacy instruction. In other words, having been trained in technical teacher education programs, they have been conditioned to accept the scientific discourse and generally fail to link theory with practice. Further, as is argued in the next chapter, a skills-driven, teach-and-test model of literacy instruction effectively removes instructional decision making from the hands of practitioners. Teachers become mere executors of the prescribed curriculum, and "the moral and ethical dimensions, not to mention the cognitive aspects of the teaching act, are submerged in a pool of standardization and conventionalism" (Kincheloe 1993, p. 21).

Researchers, too, are constrained by their own cultural limitations. Because most educational researchers are members of the privileged class and have been trained in traditional research paradigms, they generally fail to acknowledge—or even to recognize—the subjective (and hence, political) dimension of their research. Yet while it might legitimately be argued that investigations can remain "objective," it is questionable whether they can ever be "neutral" (Phillips 1993), for research designs are always conceptualized within a particular epistemological framework. In fact, as Edelsky (1991) suggests, much of our research in literacy is based upon erroneous conceptions about written language and, hence, is inherently flawed. Activities that often pass for authentic "reading" in our instruction and assessment, Edelsky argues, are merely exercises that happen to use various forms of print. Thus, while investigators may be claiming to measure reading and writing in their literacy research, they are really measuring something else (one's facility with test-taking formats, for example).

Many educational theorists who endorse a postmodern epistemology argue that researchers ought to recognize the role of perspective in science and should therefore assume a critical stance in their work (Edelsky 1991; Kincheloe 1993; McLaren and Lankshear 1993). Despite popular assumptions to the contrary, traditional educational research is ideologically constrained, having emerged within a positivistic worldview that espouses objectivism and scientific dualism. It is worth quoting the ideas of Kincheloe (1993) at length, since they reflect the basic arguments being presented here.

> No aspect of schooling is ideologically innocent; no thoughts, theories, or pedagogies are completely autonomous. Ideas, perspectives, research orientations, and the actions that come out of them are always connected to power and value interests. It is extremely difficult to understand ideological forces, their educational effects, and their influence on all researchers. Cartesian-Newtonian researchers find it particularly difficult to understand the effects of ideology—not that they are really that interested. They have often attempted to quantitatively measure ambiguous educational processes. The ideological innocence that results supports the power relations of the status quo, the mythology of classlessness, the equality of opportunity, the political neutrality of school, and the creed of financial success as a direct consequence of an individual's initiative. (p. 187)

I would argue that those who are engaged in literacy practice and research must begin to recognize that a belief in the neutrality of language and literacy is an ideological belief—one that allows us to absolve ourselves of responsibility for having to consider the ramifications of our practices. Confronting the issue of neutrality calls us to become critical by interrogating the ways in which our own ethnocentric biases determine the very questions we ask about literacy instruction, as well as how we go about seeking answers to those questions.

## CONCLUSION

Discourses are cultural representations that involve expectations for behavior and language use within particular social contexts. In this chapter, I suggest that schooled literacy is a secondary discourse that is acquired through immersion in the language of the educational institution. As social and political institutions, schools generally have promoted dominant discourses and have simultaneously embraced a technical, objective rationality that tends to obscure the political reality of literacy instruction. Prevailing practices assume that literacy can be taught as a tool or skill, devoid of cultural and ideological implications.

Three primary assumptions are examined that underlie our literacy research and pedagogy: (1) some discourses are more literate than other discourses, and hence are inherently superior; (2) practices that are founded upon scientific principles and technological rationalism are preferable to more subjective practices; and (3) it is possible for literacy instruction and research to remain neutral. Throughout this chapter, I present arguments that challenge these ideological assumptions and maintain that those of us who are engaged in literacy research and practice must begin to confront our own ethnocentric notions about language.

A standardized curriculum based upon a transmission or banking model of learning serves to control literacy instruction by defining the parameters of knowledge acquisition. Preimposed standards, content, and methodology effectively silence the voices of many of our students and deny all students the opportunity to learn perspectives that differ from their own (Delpit 1988; O'Connor 1988; Sola and Bennett 1985; Willis 1995). Giroux (1992, p. 307) writes:

> Dominant approaches to reading limit the possibilities for students to mobilize their own voices in relation to particular texts. In its dominant form, literacy is constructed in monolithic rather than pluralistic terms. Literacy becomes a matter of mastering either technical skills, information, or an elite notion of the canon.

Those students who can adapt to schooled literacy tasks typically succeed in school, whereas those whose primary discourse does not prepare them for the expectations of schooling generally fare poorly.

Thus, rather than providing a means for building upon the cultural knowledge and linguistic competence that students bring with them to school, schooled literacy tends to promote a particular form of literacy—one that inhibits creative thought and often has little personal relevance for students. Further, it affords a mechanism for sorting and labeling students, thereby providing a way for differentiating them for their future roles in school and in society. In this way, literacy instruction that is based upon a technocratic rationality not only tends to trivialize learning but may actually serve to inhibit the goal of educational equity. In the next chapter, we look at how this works by examining the consequences of schooled literacy.

## NOTES

1. I wish to emphasize that I am not advocating the elimination of Standard English instruction in our schools. It is, after all, the language of power, and to do so would be both naive and shortsighted. Rather, what I am suggesting is that linguistic variation ought to be seen as functional and legitimate, and language diversity ought to be understood and celebrated as a representation of the dynamic nature of social discourse as it is used to create meaning within the context of interpretive communities.

2. An example might be found in higher education. There is a recent trend in colleges and universities across the United States to offer special courses in Spanish to native speakers (Collison 1994). Often the emphasis in these programs is to enhance students' awareness of the social dimension of language use, that is, to teach which forms of the language are appropriate within particular social contexts, thereby expanding students' knowledge about their native language. It seems that this same approach would be valuable in teaching students about the various registers of English.

3. For example, see Bowers (1993) for a discussion of how Cartesian dualism relates to our current ecological crisis.

4. While it is perhaps erroneous to conceive of these models as being synonymous, both are based upon the assumption that knowledge can be reduced, codified, and transmitted to learners.

5. Often such marginalization is quite subtle. For instance, in a thought-provoking article, Arlette Willis (1995) describes the negative effects on her son's writing as he comes to realize that his own cultural knowledge and experiences as an African American are viewed as less significant within the educational institution than those of mainstream students.

# 3

## The Results of Schooled Literacy

The language of teachers' guides and curricular materials is a form of "talkin-about": a peculiarly stiff, jargon-ridden language of process, how to do things. It is not a language of expression or reflection. It is a language of work and technique, oriented toward achieving some narrowly (and often trivially) defined success, rather than toward achieving deeper understanding. It is about effectiveness, not truthfulness or rightness in the moral sense. It leaves little room for critical or creative thinking, little latitude for judgment. (Rexford G. Brown, *Schools of Thought*, 1991, p. 234)

The imperative to teach the basics continues to resound in nearly every classroom, school building, and legislative chamber, remnants of the reform movement of the 1980s. Rhetoric about basic skills is a battle cry frequently aimed against progressive ideas designed to challenge the status quo. Goals such as the ability to think critically and the ability to participate actively in a democracy are trivialized as they become reduced to "critical thinking skills" and "skills for effective citizenship." It is assumed that students can learn *about* critical analysis and *about* democratic participation and leave school prepared to deal with major social issues. That is, such objectives imply that students do not actually need to engage in the process of democratic participation and critical thought to be able to act responsibly in a democratic society. What skills advocates often fail to acknowledge, however, is that *process* is integrally related to *product*. That is, *process shapes thought;* the ways that we present knowledge condition and habituate us to certain patterns of thinking, certain ways of knowing, certain means of seeing and reacting to the world.

The teach-and-test syndrome that has dominated educational discourse in recent decades has blinded us to alternate realities. Culture is a human construction, and hence the dominant ideology that is reflected in the official knowledge of the school is dynamic and subject to continuous renegotiation. Yet our instructional practices—the processes we use in teaching and learning—have led to outcomes that regard culture as something static, fixed, unyielding. Society exists; our role as teachers is to train students to fit. Absent is a language of critique and possibility, a language that would lead us to explore new horizons, to conceive a different vision, to compose a more just and compassionate world.

In *Schools of Thought*, Rexford Brown (1991) argues for a "literacy of thoughtfulness," a literacy that is "imbued with the value of knowing," that engages individuals in "making meaning and negotiating it with others through reading, writing, discussion and performance" (p. 35). Thoughtfulness, in this sense, conveys both reflection and compassion; it is a literacy that "affirms the goodness of knowing" as well as "the caring about and working with others." A literacy of thoughtfulness is one that empowers. It invites dialogue and encourages critique; it promotes a sense of human agency and challenges us to create meaning in a world that often lacks imagination.

Schooled literacy, on the other hand, promotes acquiescence. Textbooks and instructional guides govern classroom discourse; absent is a sense of enablement, an affirmation of autonomy, a nurturing of passion and intellect. The language of school is a language of control—one that discourages alternative visions and that denies the cultural experiences of many of our students.

I argue throughout this chapter that this language of control can have unfortunate consequences for both schools and society. I suggest that the marginalization of the cultural experiences of minority groups can create tremendous tensions in students' lives as they attempt to accommodate the value system of the school with their own cultural beliefs and linguistic styles, thereby perpetuating a system of educational failure and oppression. Further, a discourse that promotes dependency and passivity can have serious repercussions within a democracy, whose very existence depends upon the active vigilance of an educated and empowered citizenry.

In the pages that follow, the effects of schooled literacy are examined. I show how our quest for neutrality and scientifically determined curricula often leads to ways of framing instruction that effectively control both teachers and students. The resulting erosion of professional autonomy and our emphasis upon reified knowledge has led to indifference, and this indifference must be confronted if we are to thrive as a multiracial and multicultural democracy. At the conclusion of this chapter, I argue for a more critical, proper literacy—one that encourages thoughtfulness and promotes the communicative competence necessary for democratic empowerment.

## SCHOOLED LITERACY AND THE CONTROL OF TEACHERS

The rationalization of school-based knowledge has subjected teachers to increased technical control, that is, control that is incorporated into the structure of one's work. The high-status symbolism associated with the standard curriculum (e.g., scientific management systems) creates the illusion that teachers' professional status is being enhanced. Many have observed that what is actually occurring, however, is that teachers' instructional authority is being systematically eroded, as instructional decisions are increasingly coming under the control of commercial publishers and state officials (Apple 1988, 1993a, 1993b; Freedman, Jackson, and Boles 1983; Shannon 1989). Rather than playing a central role in instructional planning, teachers have become mere executors of "scripted lessons" (Erickson 1984, p. 534) provided for them in the prepackaged curriculum.

This deskilling of teachers, however, not only involves the erosion of teachers' authority in decision making. It also involves a form of intellectual deskilling "in which mental workers are cut off from their own fields and again must rely even more heavily on ideas and processes provided by 'experts'" (Apple 1988, p. 42). Like other workers whose professional autonomy has fallen victim to the reductionist management system of Taylorism, teachers have become conditioned to comply with their restricted role as their work has become increasingly controlled by prescriptive policies and programs. The real danger is that skills that were at one time essential to the craft of teaching (e.g., setting curricular goals, individualizing instruction based upon students' needs and cultural expectations, establishing content, etc.) will begin to atrophy as curriculum planning remains essentially outside of their domain (Apple and Jungck 1993).

In his 1990 Presidential Address to the National Reading Conference, Gerald Duffy discusses these concerns and suggests that literacy experts contribute to the deskilling and subsequent disempowerment of teachers.

> The problem is in the perception—on the part of teachers and those of us trying to help teachers—that instructional power lies not with the minds of teachers but, rather, with programs, procedures, or theories that we create for teachers to follow. . . . we are participating in a system which encourages teachers to compliantly follow rather than to take charge. . . . when we take control away from [teachers] by directing them to follow materials or codified approaches or tested procedures, we make them into technicians who follow directions. In doing so, we rob them of their professional dignity. (1991, pp. 3–5)

With the standardization of the processes and products of instruction, teachers become even less capable of critically evaluating their positions as educators and of engaging in reflective praxis that would lead to change. In essence, teachers (as well as students) become victims of their instructional programs; they passively sift through textbooks, worksheets, and workbooks while giving little thought to the consequences of their actions (Shannon 1989). In fact, often schools have placed increasing demands upon teachers to accomplish more in the same amount of (or less) time, making them even more dependent upon prepackaged curricula. Caught up in the daily reality of their managerial roles, they are less able to function as "transformative intellectuals" (Aronowitz and Giroux 1985; Giroux 1988) and essentially become purveyors of mainstream thought.[1]

Kincheloe (1991) suggests that teachers are actually engaged in what he calls "bad work"—work that has emerged from modernist assumptions of bureaucratization and scientific rationalism. "Bad work" impels teachers to be managers of a predefined curricula, and their efforts must be intensified in order to "cover the material." Such work subjugates human nurturing and long-term social welfare to the goals of efficiency and productivity. In other words, work becomes separated from life: "laborers and teachers see little connection between their work lives and the needs and concerns of the human community" (p. 9). Kincheloe argues that, in order to promote democratic principles and combat the increasing technical control of teachers, schools must pursue what he calls "good work." "Good work" gives teachers professional autonomy and encourages them to undertake critical research so that they might engage in informed praxis. At the same time, it limits tedious and repetitive management tasks and allows them to reconceptualize their work so that they might contribute to the social good.

Managed curricula not only affects teachers' control of their craft, but it also affects the interpersonal relationships between teachers and learners. In discussing his research conducted at a Midwestern elementary school, Gitlin (1983) describes the results of technical control in the classrooms he observed:

> Teachers . . . were somewhat "disconnected" from the students because of their involvement with bureaucratic tasks such as checking and recording post-tests. This made it difficult for them to use their personal knowledge to relate to students, leaving them less opportunity to confront the priorities and values that filtered through the curriculum. This could only minimize their ability to act in a transformative way. (p. 210)

As a result of a preoccupation with managed curricula, meaningful dialogue that might lead students and teachers to consciously reflect on their own perspectives and values gets omitted in favor of covering course objectives and simply "getting through the textbook." The use of a rationalized curricula often results in depersonalized instruction, with teachers basing their instructional decisions upon skill and content deficiencies—as assessed by criteria relating to the textbook and the management system—rather than upon the genuine needs of their students. Interaction is reduced to getting through the lesson, which militates against creating an uninhibiting, collaborative environment where students are supported and their ideas legitimated.

What often occurs in such classrooms is an erosion of the trusting relationships that are essential for learning. Real learning often emerges from confusion and error, and therefore it involves vulnerability. Hence, students must feel secure and accepted within the learning environment before they are willing to take risks. In other words, students must feel that their attempts are significant and their knowledge is valued—that they are affirmed as partners in the learning process. Managed curriculum, however, reinforces a particular view of reality, and learning becomes a matter of arriving at so-called correct answers, rather than exploring diverse possibilities. Having been conditioned to a system that marginalizes their cultural knowledge and that denies alternate interpretations, students often become skeptical of the official knowledge that is being offered to them, and consequently they begin to distrust the expert who represents that knowledge. Rather than becoming a community of learners, the classroom often becomes the site of contestation, with teachers and students in opposite corners. Further, because few opportunities are provided for students to demonstrate their competence, they (or their parents, or their home environments) are often blamed for educational failure that is, in actuality, the result of many complex factors—not the least of which is a curriculum that alienates rather than affirms.

## SCHOOLED LITERACY AND THE CONTROL OF STUDENTS

Instructional management systems, that is, curricular materials that are designed to teach the skills of literacy through incorporating basic scientific principles, can have a negative effect on students as well as teachers. As discussed in chapter 2, such skills packages appear to be scientific because what is taught can be easily organized and quantified; further, the teaching of product-oriented literacy skills has the appearance of maintaining impartiality. Yet it is precisely because isolated subskills are so easily measured—and instructional conformity is encouraged and facilitated—that the skills model of instruction is, in reality, highly political. Textbooks, too, exert control in a variety of ways, by defining what content is of most worth and by promoting ritualized responses that are consistent with a transmission model of learning. In this section, the ways in which power is exercised through both (1) the control of knowledge and (2) the control of classroom discourse are examined in more detail.

### Control of Knowledge

There are a number of ways in which schooled literacy tends to marginalize the cultural knowledge of students and hence control the reproduction of knowledge in our society. This marginalization occurs explicitly, through the obvious omission and distortion of the historical and cultural experiences of minorities and other disenfranchised groups, and implicitly, through the material forms used in instruction.

Sleeter and Grant (1991) differentiate between "cultural" or "regenerative" knowledge and the "reified" knowledge of the school. Regenerative knowledge is community based; it derives its meaning from the beliefs, behaviors, and cultural experiences of those who create it. Reified knowledge, on the other hand, is abstract and codified; it has been "encoded for transmission, and in the process decontextualized and converted to a static product" (p. 52). In literacy instruction, reified knowledge—manifested through the managed curriculum and the static images presented in textbooks—tends to remove the locus of control from both teachers and students. Hence students' cultural/regenerative knowledge is rendered insignificant and remains outside the periphery of real knowledge.

Let us consider, for example, the indirect regulation of official knowledge through textbook use. Because textbooks represent particular interests and definitions of reality, they have been the source of considerable controversy over the years, and various groups have vied for cultural inclusion. Such inclusion, however, generally results in what Apple (1993a 1993b) calls "mentioning," whereby information that would benefit disenfranchised groups is given cursory exposure but is not developed in depth. An example of this "mentioning" phenomenon is described by Harris (1992), who notes that popular books for children on the story of Christopher Columbus "mention" the reality of the death and enslavement of millions of Native Americans, yet they "bury it amidst the mass of other information, a strategy that implicitly tells us that mass murder is not that important" (p. 27). By merely adding such information but minimizing its significance, the knowledge of dominant groups maintains its legitimacy and the cultural, regenerative knowledge of subordinate groups is subsumed within the official knowledge of the school.

Perhaps nowhere is such cultural hegemony more evident than in the work of E. D. Hirsch (1987). Hirsch argues for a "cultural literacy" that would enable students to comprehend the "content" of various disciplines. The cultural literacy that he advocates, however, does not include the culture of nonmainstream populations but rather that of the dominant European American society. This ideology is also reflected in the emphasis upon a common curriculum or "canon" that is designed to promote national unity and cultural integration, while obscuring the privileged status of its content (Banks 1991; Hollins and Spencer 1990).

Textbooks, therefore, are really "a form of cultural politics" (Apple 1993b, p. 53). Texts represent a history of struggle and controversy—a competition over what constitutes official knowledge, an ongoing contest to determine whose voices will be legitimated and whose will be silenced. Apple (1993b, p. 52) writes:

All of these controversies are not "simply" about the content of the books students find—or don't find—in their schools, though obviously they are about that as well. The issues also involve profoundly different definitions of the common good, about our society and where it should be heading, about cultural visions, and about our children's future.

As discussed in previous chapters, literacy is socially and culturally defined. Hence, one might argue that those who have the power to determine what constitutes the good life at any point in time also have the power to determine what knowledge and skills are required to get us there.

While it is evident that the cultural experiences of many of our students are excluded in the official curriculum, the process of knowledge selection is an overt practice, one that can be (and frequently is) challenged. Yet schooled literacy also marginalizes students' cultural experiences in implicit and subtle ways, through the actual structure and design of the materials used for instruction. In other words, knowledge control is not only manifested in *what* content is available to students, but also in *how* that content is presented—in the *process* of language use. Consider, for instance, the materials that are typically used for teaching the skills of written language. In an effort to maintain the semblance of neutrality, students' literacy experiences are reduced to accomplishing a series of fragmented tasks, and progress subsequently is gauged according to their ability to master a certain set of measurable indices. Teaching and testing the components of written language become the primary objectives for the literacy program. Absent are opportunities for students to use their cultural knowledge or to demonstrate their linguistic competence in authentic social contexts. Rather, students must conform to a set of narrow, predetermined criteria. Those who can readily master this reified knowledge are generally placed in the high-ability groups, whereas those who find such rote learning difficult will generally remain in the low-ability groups. Research documents that children in low-ability groups typically receive less instructional time and more work in basic skills than their higher-achieving counterparts, thereby perpetuating their already inferior status (Allington 1991; Bennett 1991; Hiebert and Fisher 1991). Since it has been found that reading instructional groups and academic tracks can often be differentiated along lines of class and culture, our dependence upon skills instruction and the subsequent evaluation of those skills serves to reinforce and legitimate the system of social stratification that already exists in schools (Edelsky 1991; Grant and Rothenberg 1986; Moll and Diaz 1987; Oakes 1985; Rist 1970).

Like the programs used for written language development, textbooks, too, control how content is delivered by segmenting knowledge and presenting it in a static, linear fashion. Such nonintegrated knowledge can be readily transmitted and quantified, thereby facilitating accountability. Luke (1988) suggests that textbooks can be thought of as "closed texts" that "constrain readers to a narrow set of interpretive options" through the use of a simplified semantic structure (p. 39). Students are taught that the official knowledge of the text has only one legitimate interpretation, and all other interpretations are to be discounted. Instruction often consists of providing students with tactics that will enable them to comprehend the text, that is, strategies that will help them to arrive at the proper responses to the questions being posed by the teacher, the textbook, or the test.[2]

It has been found that teachers also contribute to the process of knowledge reduction through the ways they present information to students. In *Contradictions of Control* (1988), Linda McNeil shows how teachers intentionally control knowledge in an effort to reduce conflict in their classrooms. This control is accomplished by reducing the content to a series of lists, or refusing to explore a subject in depth, thereby fragmenting and mystifying topics of study. Framed within a transmission or banking model of instruction, such tactics function to control student behavior by controlling their access to knowledge. She writes:

> What is clear is that where knowledge control is used as a form of classroom control, alienation increases for all participants, further reinforcing patterns of control. . . . One real effect of the alienation students feel toward school-supplied information is the opportunity cost of rejecting much course content without having any sense of how to find (or generate or evaluate) credible information on their own. (p. 188)

As the result of such pedagogical tactics, McNeil suggests, students develop a "client mentality" whereby they strive to get through school by expending the least amount of effort, while at the same time expressing the vague hope that "someday . . . they will teach us . . . what we need to know" (1988, p. 79).

To summarize, the reductionist view associated with schooled literacy has been criticized for inhibiting creative thought and promoting singular, mechanical responses, thereby eroding the ability of students to maintain ownership of their learning. The very structure of the traditional standardized curriculum used in instruction can force students to perform according to a series of ritualized and previously defined rules—rules determined by those in power (Perry and Fraser 1993). Further, through the process of learning reified knowledge, students acquire the myth that complicated issues can be reduced to simplistic topics, and that there are absolute, unified answers to questions that, in reality, often demand complex and divergent responses.

## Control of Classroom Discourse

Managed instructional programs not only control content, but they also tend to govern interaction within the classroom. The basic premise underlying the transmission or banking model upon which current instructional practices are based is that the role of the teacher/expert is to impart or transmit skills and knowledge to the student/learner. The teacher assumes the primary responsibility for learning; students are passive recipients of school-based knowledge. Consequently, students are given relatively few opportunities to interact in meaningful ways. In a fifteen-year longitudinal study, Gordon Wells (1986) compared the functions and quantity of language use found in the home and in school. Relatively few differences were found in categories related to the form and function of language; rather, the primary differences that were found related to the degree of language use. In the home, children engaged in conversation about as much as adults. In school, however, there was a significant imbalance in favor of teacher-talk. Wells concludes that

> Most significant of all in explaining the generally reduced level of [linguistic] competence that children show at school is the much more dominating role that teachers play in conversation. . . . Small wonder that some children have little to say or even appear to be lacking in conversational skills altogether. As repeatedly emphasized, conversation is a reciprocal activity; the more one participant dominates, the more the opportunities for the other participant to make his or her own personal contribution are reduced and constrained. (p. 87)

The transmission model can be contrasted with the "reciprocal interaction" or "collaborative" model (Cummins 1986; Wells 1986, 1988), which assumes that learning requires interaction in order to construct meaning. The reciprocal interaction model encourages genuine dialogue whereby ideas are challenged and negotiated. Hence, a nonneutral stance is openly sought and acknowledged, and the integration of students' cultural/regenerative knowledge with new concepts and ideas becomes central.

Research shows that there are particular discourse patterns that ensue from the transmission view of learning, and these patterns result in limited opportunities for expanding students' linguistic competence. For instance, Bloome and Nieto (1992) discuss the language associated with the use of basal reading programs—a form of language they refer to as "basalese." Basalese uses a particular prosodic style that is characterized by monotone and word-by-word rendition, which is accomplished in a steady rhythmic pattern. In addition, basalese requires exact reproduction of the text in both oral reading and oral response situations; even meaningful deviations are discouraged. In other research, David Bloome (1987) has noted the prevalence of "text reproduction" in using content area texts, which is a way of interpreting and interacting with print with the intention of reconstructing (rather than challenging) the essential information found in a textbook. Text reproduction is related to "procedural display," whereby the primary goal is to complete a standard interactional pattern in order to move the lesson forward.

Tharp and Gallimore (1991) refer to such discourse patterns as "recitation" and suggest that this style of interaction is still prevalent in American schools.

Newer versions of the recitation pattern are presented in the form of predetermined "scripts," which emphasize "rote learning and student passivity, facts and low-level questions, and low-level cognitive functions" (p. 1). The main function of these ritualized patterns of discourse is to control interaction (and hence to control the information acquired) rather than to promote meaningful dialogue (or what Tharp and Gallimore call "instructional conversations") between teachers and students. Accuracy is stressed over risk taking, and classroom discourse typically involves producing precise displays of knowledge in response to teacher-generated questions and building the teacher's meanings ("guess-what's-in-the-teacher's-head"), versus active collaboration between teacher and learner (Cazden 1988).

By controlling classroom discourse, the scripted, sequential lessons associated with managed instructional programs can actually hinder the development of acceptable linguistic forms by minority students. Interaction is essential to the acquisition of secondary discourses, yet students are given few opportunities either to interact with others in the classroom setting, or to interact with meaningful texts in order to acquire new language structures. Instead, as Gee (1989) has suggested, a rationalized curriculum emphasizes the superficial features of literacy and language use, without giving students real reading and writing experiences that might enable them to apply their emerging understandings about language. Because they are not actively engaged in their own learning, students have few opportunities to display their linguistic competence and to use the knowledge and experiences of their home culture, and consequently teachers almost invariably underestimate children's capabilities (Cook- Gumperz 1986; Wells 1986). Hence, the predominant instructional model can have particularly adverse effects on disadvantaged minority students, since students' behaviors may provide evidence that reinforces teachers' limited expectations (Gilmore 1987, 1992; Wells 1986).

## THE REPERCUSSIONS OF CONTROL

By controlling knowledge and thereby hindering language development and denying students' cultural and linguistic experiences, schooled literacy can potentially have two other undesirable outcomes: student apathy, demonstrated through passivity and acquiescence; and active resistance to schooling, demonstrated through subversive action or through dropping out.

### Student Apathy

When skills and facts are seen as ends in themselves that can only be mastered through direct instruction, students assume dependent roles and are generally only minimally engaged in the learning process. Edelsky (1991) observes that many of our literacy practices position students as "objects" that are acted upon rather than as "subjects" who maintain ownership of the literacy event (also see Freire and Macedo 1987). This notion is similar to that of McNeil (1988), who suggests that the transmission of superficial content relegates students to the position of "client." The role of client or object requires only a limited investment in learning. Further, as has been previously emphasized, external control of what is learned and how it is learned marginalizes the linguistic competence and cultural knowledge students bring with them to school. Consequently, rather than promoting a pedagogy that is empowering—that is, one that encourages students to become active generators of knowledge—schooled literacy actually hinders development of the confidence and motivation necessary for academic success (Cummins 1986; Kohn 1993). Hence, the results of a transmitted, rationalized curriculum can have particularly undesirable effects on those students who are members of minority or disadvantaged groups.

Kohn (1993) notes that denying students ownership in the instructional setting can result in student burnout. Lacking control of their own learning, students try to overcome their sense of powerlessness by becoming apathetic, meeting only the minimum requirements in order to get by.[3] He writes:

> Much of what is disturbing about students' attitudes and behavior may be a function of the fact that they have little to say about what happens to them all day. They are compelled to follow someone else's rules, study someone else's curriculum, and submit continually to someone else's evaluation. The mystery, really, is not that so many students are indifferent about what they have to do in school but that any of them are not. (1993, p. 10)

Kohn goes on to argue that a pedagogy that legitimizes students' voices and permits active participation and negotiation develops in students higher self-esteem, greater motivation, and a sense of academic competence.

Maxine Greene writes passionately about the kinds of institutional and instructional practices that tend to control and dehumanize students. In *Landscapes of Learning* (1978), Maxine Greene argues that, rather than educating individuals who can engage in critical reflection and who possess the determination necessary for responsible civic action, we are producing citizens who are basically lethargic—citizens who lack what she refers to as "wideawakedness":

> The dominant preoccupation, from the days of the founding of the public schools to the present moment, has been with what Horace Mann called "dominion and supremacy over the appetites and passions—during the docile and teachable years of childhood." There have been exceptions, of course, but contemporary observers, like Charles Silberman and others, still find life in classrooms characterized by "values of docility, passivity, conformity, and lack of

trust." The call for a return to "basics," the dismay over presumably falling test scores, and the troubled preoccupation with "discipline" are likely to lead to more passivity as new kinds of "order" are imposed. (p. 113)

Because the underlying ideological assumptions of schools tend to promote powerlessness, Greene states that students "appear to have two alternatives: to submit or to break free, which means going it on their own" (p. 114).

Greene suggests that knowledge control militates against the development of "wideawakedness" and hence is a form of oppression that can hinder the development of a moral imperative necessary for transformative action. By confining students' experiences and defining what is to count as "knowledge," the prevalent model of education and literacy in schools tends to "subject human beings to technical systems, deprive them of spontaneity, and erode their self-determination, their autonomy" (p. 100).

I would suggest that treating students as clients or objects to be manipulated and controlled, and denying the appetites and passions of young learners, reflects an underlying ideology that counteracts our professed democratic ideals. Literacy is seen as a technological tool used merely for transmitting seemingly neutral information, and students become products on the educational assembly line—empty vessels who have been habituated to respond passively and conditioned to acquiesce to those in authority. Thus, while student submission might facilitate behavioral control by keeping them in their place, at the same time it fosters powerlessness and dependency—characteristics that have seemingly left us paralyzed as citizens to act in the face of major social problems. We might be challenged to look more carefully at this hidden curriculum and ask, as Sirotnik (1988, p. 56) does, "Is this the way we want it?"

### Active Resistance

Some students are content to resist passively by remaining minimally engaged with schooled literacy tasks. Others, however, resort to active resistance, either through subversive action or through dropping out. Such resistance is frequently associated with minority populations and students who are considered to be at risk, whose cultural and linguistic experiences often do not coincide with the expectations of the school. To better understand this discussion, it becomes necessary to explore why some students tend to resist schooled literacy more than others.

Ogbu (1987, 1990) distinguishes between voluntary or "immigrant" minorities, that is, those who have willingly become members of a society for economic, political, or social gain, and involuntary or "castelike" minorities, identifiable subpopulations incorporated into a society against their will. Historically, involuntary minorities have been oppressed in our society both instrumentally, through inequality within the labor force, and expressively, by being ascribed undesirable traits and characteristics. Therefore, minority students tend to oppose the school's attempts at acculturation and prefer instead the security and social identity of their own culture. Such opposition often leads to the rejection of particular styles, behaviors, and ways of speaking associated with school and with acting White, in favor of maintaining certain markers of cultural identity and group solidarity (Davidson 1996; Erickson 1987; Gumperz 1985; Helms 1993; MacLeod 1987, 1995; Ogbu 1987; Willis 1977). Loyalty to one's cultural or ethnic peer group can also lead to a rejection of reading and writing, since becoming literate (i.e., "educated") may be interpreted as joining the opposing camp (Kohl 1995; McDermott 1974; D. M. Smith 1986).

An example of social resistance can be found in the work of Gilmore (1987, 1992), who conducted a three-year study in a predominantly African American urban elementary school. The purpose of the investigation was to examine the factors involved in students' differential access to literacy. Gilmore found that the primary determining factor for entrance into the elite Academics Plus Program was "attitude," a characteristic defined by certain behavioral displays. The two primary features of Black communicative style examined in the study were "stylized sulking" and "doin' steps." Stylized sulking was an individual response to authority that consisted of a nonverbal display of defiance. "Steps" consisted of choreographed chants that were accepted within the community but were seen by the school as "disrespectful" and "too sexual" and therefore were deemed inappropriate by the educational establishment. Gilmore's work shows that such verbal and nonverbal displays serve as cultural markers that can have a negative effect on students' access to literacy. Those students whose verbal and nonverbal behaviors coincided with the expectations of the school were assigned to Academic Plus, whereas those students who exhibited primarily Black discourse responses were determined to have a "bad attitude" and were subsequently denied entrance. Gilmore traces the roots of these stylized responses, observing that "sulking" and "stepping" parallel the action of slaves in American history:

> The images of sulking and stepping youngsters suggests that we may not have come very far in our own brand of modern-day racism. Young students show their resistance to the authority in control through sulking facial gestures and body language, though they may go through the motions of their expected behaviors. Steps are reminiscent of some of the slave songs, sung almost in code, so that slave masters would not be able to comprehend the real content of their messages. (1992, p. 125)

Hence, just as slaves used such nonthreatening forms of opposition against those who had power over them, Gilmore suggests that these sullen displays and musical expressions might still be viewed as acts of resistance to the dominant ideology found in schools.

Minority status is not the only variable associated with resistance to schooling and to schooled literacy. Social class can also be a major determining factor. In fact, it has been found that socioeconomic status is the most consistent indicator in predicting success or failure in school (Vacha and McLaughlin 1992). An example of how class conflict leads to student resistance can be found in the work of Paul Willis (1977). Willis shows how a group of English working-class lads resisted the formal school structure by creating an informal counterschool culture, a culture marked by defiance and by various behaviors typically exhibited by working-class laborers on the shop floor. Thus, Willis concludes, inadequate school performance is due not only to the symbolic attachment of the educational establishment to the oppressive forces of society, but it is also due to students' response to this oppression, which "makes them more or less accomplices to their own school success or failure" (Ogbu 1987, p. 317).[4]

Dropping out of school is perhaps the ultimate resistance to schooling, in that it represents a conclusive and overt rejection of the educational institution. Statistics reveal that persons of color and those of low socioeconomic status tend to leave school in disproportionately greater numbers than their middle-class Anglo counterparts. For instance, recent national reports indicate that both African Americans and Hispanics continue to have substantially higher dropout rates than Whites (*Facts on File* 1993, 1995).[5] A 1986 report of the Children's Defense Fund states that "regardless of race, students from poor families are three to four times more likely to drop out than those from more affluent households" (p. 223; reported in Taylor and Dorsey-Gaines 1988, p. 197). Such findings are particularly disturbing given the changing demographics in the United States. A recent report states that minority students currently comprise the majority in seventeen of twenty-five of America's largest urban school districts and, according to some estimates, approximately one-half of Black and Hispanic youth will be socioeconomically disadvantaged by the year 2010 (Cohen 1993; Heflin 1991). Clearly, we can no longer ignore the problem of persistent poverty in our country.[6]

In her book entitled *Framing Dropouts* (1991), Michelle Fine traces the lives of students in an urban high school in upper Manhattan and examines their large-scale rejection of the educational institution. In this school, Fine found that 87 percent of the students left school or were discharged between ninth grade entrance and graduation. While some went on to pursue a GED, 66 percent never returned to school. The stories of these students reveal institutional policies that actually promote mass exodus. These include (1) a narrow and essentially irrelevant curriculum, which tends to silence students and ultimately leads to boredom and frustration; (2) student retention, or being left back, which "may offer the final justification to give in, to acknowledge defeat, and to surrender to the pressures of poverty and family need" (p. 74); (3) the failure of schools to confront and adapt to family problems, such as student pregnancy, family violence, or the need to contribute to the family's economy; and (4) coercive discharge, a practice of school expulsion that ironically was supported in this school by financial incentives. Hence, as Fine and others have suggested, it is probably erroneous to speak of students as *dropouts,* for in actuality they have been pushed out of our educational institutions that are designed to serve dominant Eurocentric interests. She writes:

> From inside the school, the discharge process appears to most, as inevitable, necessary, and nondisruptive. But, would this process appear inevitable, necessary, and nondisruptive if 66 percent of white middle-class students were discharged from a ninth-grade cohort? If almost one-third of a school were disappeared between September and June? Or would the process and the structures that support it, grow suspect for collusion in the perpetuation of social injustice? If silencing exports critique, discharge dispenses with bodies. (p. 69)

Given this bleak scenario, I suggest that schooling in general, and literacy instruction in particular, require that we make *moral* choices—choices relating to whether students' voices ought to be dismissed, whether students' lives are indeed expendable. It is apparent that, at least in many of our schools, students are viewed as either assets or liabilities, depending upon their particular cultural capital. When persons are considered to be problems for the system *by the very system commissioned to serve them,* then something has gone seriously awry. Again, we must ask fundamental questions about literacy and schooling, questions that get at the heart of whose interests schools serve, and the role of education and literacy in a nation that claims to promote equity.

## CONCLUSION

In this and previous chapters, I argue that literacy teaching and research are not neutral enterprises. Rather, there are particular ideological perspectives that frame our practices, leading to a form of literacy that I have chosen to call *schooled literacy.* Schooled literacy is the literacy that counts in schools. It is characterized by standardized oral and written discourse patterns and a reified, scientifically managed curriculum that can be readily transmitted and assessed. I have also argued that schooled literacy—through regulating the products and processes of knowledge acquisition—controls both teachers and students, thereby resulting in the deskilling of teachers and leading to various patterns of apathy and resistance among students. The negative effects of schooled literacy particularly can be felt by nonmainstream students, who tend to be marginalized and alienated through the dominant discourses associated with schooling.

A number of theorists have suggested that schooling practices designed to control rather than to empower can undermine the realization of a genuine democracy. George Wood (1988) contrasts the Jeffersonian notion of a participatory democracy with our current protectionist democratic system and notes that the original vision for our democratic society was one that required active citizen participation. He suggests that, within our representative system, apathy has a definite function in that it maintains the illusion of satisfaction with the status quo and "keep[s] to a minimum the demands upon the system" (p. 169). Wood goes on to state that the scientific management ethos in schools tends to restrict democratic involvement in that it encourages acquiescence and gives control primarily to those outside the classroom. Hence, instruction that inhibits collaborative and critical inquiry prepares students for a protectionist democracy rather than a true participatory democracy by promoting habits of dependence and indifference. Students absorb the message that their lives are to be regulated and managed by others—that culture is something that is received, not created.

Conceptions that view literacy as a form of technology tend to conceal the process whereby dominant cultural beliefs become embedded in instructional practice. Absent is any real reflection on the potential of literacy for changing one's life chances, for establishing a more just society, or for generating "possibilities for individual and social emancipation" (Giroux 1988, p. 18). As Purpel (1989) reminds us, culture is not something that is fixed and static; rather, it is a human construction and therefore can be reconstituted and transformed. Currently, schools primarily function to acculturate, that is, to transmit and preserve various cultural images and values. What is required, Purpel suggests, are educational institutions that will assume the leadership necessary for creating a new social vision, that is, schools that take seriously their role to "educate about what our culture is while helping to redefine it" (p. 11).

The power to act—to redefine and transform the culture—requires that individuals have a sense of control over their own destinies (Banks 1991). By ignoring the social and cultural (and hence, political) dimensions of literacy, however, schools succeed in conveying the notion that literacy has no meaning beyond a certain narrow or functional level. Schooled literacy therefore becomes what Lankshear and Lawler (1987) have called an "improper" literacy, that is, a literacy that reduces one's capacity for control, a literacy that renders us invisible and therefore powerless. An improper literacy can be contrasted with a "proper" literacy—a literacy that "enhances people's control over their lives and their capacity for dealing rationally with decisions by enabling them to identify, understand, and act to transform, social relationships and practices in which power is structured unequally" (p. 74). A proper literacy demands that both students and educators learn how to "read the world" at the same time they "read the word" (Freire and Macedo 1987), and that the word be a part of their own lived experiences.

As educators, then, we must recognize that we are responsible for transmitting culture, yet we are also responsible for helping to transform it. To this end, we must interrogate our own values about literacy and schooling and must begin to ask ourselves the truly important questions, such as why are we educating, and whose purposes does education serve? As I argue in the next several chapters, educational reform requires that we invoke a critical imagination about the kind of society we want and how we intend to get there.

# NOTES

1. It is important to note that teachers resist this control in various ways. Thus, while the goal of standardized, managed curricula may be to make instructional materials essentially teacher-proof, instructional conformity is never really achieved. See Gail McCutcheon (1988) for an excellent discussion on the ways that the curriculum becomes enacted in classrooms.

2. It is acknowledged that attempts are being made to improve standardized tests to include more authentic literacy tasks. Yet our system of accountability remains problematic for a number of reasons, primarily because there is a failure to consider the social and cultural dimensions of language use. For an excellent critique of current testing practices, see Edelsky (1991).

3. Shor and Freire (1987) refer to this type of behavior as "passive/aggressive." Eventually, many students will resist all attempts to educate them by refusing to engage in any meaningful discourse or critical debate.

4. Another important ethnographic study on student resistance to school is Jay MacLeod's *Ain't No Makin' It* (1987). MacLeod investigated the lives of two groups of high school boys living in low-income projects and compared their responses to schooling. Ironically, the group that was most responsive to schooling consisted primarily of African Americans, whereas the predominantly Anglo group largely rejected school, despite the many programs provided for "at risk" populations. A more recent edition of this volume (1995) documents the lives of these students after high school and provides a graphic and provocative account of the deleterious results of classism in American society.

5. According to a report issued by the U.S. Department of Education and released in the fall of 1992, the dropout rate among 16-to-24-year-old Hispanics had increased to 35.3 percent in 1991 from a previous figure of 34.3 percent in 1972. For these same years, the dropout rate for Blacks in the same age category had declined to 13.6 percent from 21.3 percent. This rate is still considerably higher than that of Whites, which was found to be 8.9 percent (*Facts on File Yearbook* 1993).

6. Recent statistics issued by the United Nations Children's Fund are also cause for alarm. These findings indicate that the percentage of children living in poverty in the United States is over 20 percent, more than double that of any other industrialized nation ("Children in Poverty" 1993).

# 4

## Realizing a Democratic Vision

The retreat from democracy is also evident in the absence of serious talk about how as a nation we might educate future generations in the language and practice of moral compassion, critical agency, and the utopian horizons of social imagination. The discourse of leadership appears trapped in a vocabulary in which the estimate of a good society is expressed in indices that measure markets, defense systems, and the Gross National Product. Missing in this discourse is a vocabulary for talking about and creating democratic public cultures and communities that are attentive to the problems of homelessness, hunger, censorship, media manipulation, and the rampant individualism and greed that . . . has become the hallmark of the last decade. (Henry Giroux, *Living Dangerously*, 1993, p. 11)

Organized education is to be seen not predominately in the service of scholarship nor primarily to serve the state or the economy but primarily to serve the task of nurturing, nourishing, and sustaining the quest to meet our highest aspirations and most profound commitments. The standards of a society and culture (and hence of its educational institutions) involve concerns for the degree of freedom, equality, justice, and fulfillment enjoyed by its members. (David Purpel, "Holistic Education in a Prophetic Voice," 1993, pp. 79–80)

Perhaps the greatest measure of a civilized society is the degree of compassion it has for its disenfranchised and dispossessed members. Embedded within our historical traditions is a belief in the inherent dignity and worth of all of humanity, a worth that endows every individual with certain inalienable rights—the right to life, liberty, and the pursuit of happiness. While such rhetoric rings hollow for many of our citizens, it nonetheless has become a part of our collective memory. It has become translated into a democratic vision, a quest for equity, a goal to which we might aspire. This vision has been the driving force behind countless struggles, from the struggle to emancipate those within our borders who are in bondage, to the continuing pursuit of political and economic parity among women, persons of color, and other marginalized groups.

Yet, in many ways, this vision has become obscured, and schools have contributed to its erosion. Couched in the language of accountability and neutrality, recent reform movements have failed to address those conditions and structures in society that perpetuate injustice and oppression. A quest for higher test scores, longer school days, and a basic curriculum has dominated contemporary reform movements; absent in the reform discourse is an honest interrogation of the kind of society we would like to have. In other words, our democratic vision—the pursuit of liberty and justice for all—has become overshadowed by our need to remain competitive within a global economy. Attempts to address the moral decay of our society are typically reduced to simplistic solutions, such as the introduction of prayer in the schools, corporal punishment, and school vouchers. What such recommendations fail to acknowledge is that, for justice and equity to be realized, our society requires not reformation, but transformation. For schools to contribute to this transformation, we must reexamine the purposes of schooling and reaffirm our commitment to the democratic principles upon which this nation was founded.

Our society is becoming increasingly pluralistic, and hence the quest for freedom and justice for all perhaps becomes an even greater challenge. Our conceptualization of democracy must be one that is a "multicultural, multiracial democracy" (Perry and Fraser 1993), one that encourages the civic involvement of all of our nation's citizenry—women, persons of color, those who are impoverished, the physically challenged, persons who are regarded as lower class. A genuine democratic state involves the sharing of power and the active participation of all citizens (Banks 1997). This participatory democracy can be contrasted with a representative or protectionist form of democracy, where power is unevenly distributed and citizens are involved in political action primarily through the election process (Barber 1984; Wood 1988).

A participatory democracy—one that promotes the equal sharing of power—goes beyond the notion of equal opportunity by demanding equity. That is, a democratic ideal does not merely require that all have a chance to acquire upward mobility. Rather, it requires that all have a voice in the active process of deliberation and debate—in determining our common destiny, in defining the common good, in shaping our collective future. Hence, students must be prepared to communicate effectively and to live harmoniously with those who are different from themselves. The concept of equity involves a different form of discourse; it requires a discourse that goes beyond mere tolerance, and that requires us to become actively engaged in learning from one another so that human understanding and human effectiveness might be enhanced.

In order to realize a strong or participatory democracy, language and literacy must be seen as a means for empowerment. A participatory democracy requires that students become "properly literate" (Lankshear and Lawler

1987); that is, they must be able to use literacy to enhance their control over their own lives so that they might be able to confront those conditions that hinder the equal sharing of power. A proper literacy includes the requisite for developing both oral and written competence, so that students might be able to use language in a range of social settings. In other words, students must be able to use both written and spoken language to communicate in various social contexts, to engage in critical dialogue, and to make their views known.

At the same time, empowerment, as Barber (1992) argues, should not merely involve the freedom to share opinions and ideas. Rather, civic participation necessitates an agreement upon common principles and a commitment to shared understandings. Hence, the discourse promoted through literacy instruction ought to be a moral discourse—one that strives to overcome prejudice, to defy elitism, and to develop a more equitable and compassionate society. Barber writes that the ultimate goal of "schoolroom speech" is "moral growth and the development of autonomous, empathetic, critical human beings capable of genuinely free speech in a world of power into which they will eventually be delivered—ready or not" (p. 97).

This chapter provides a framework for conceptualizing literacy instruction in a democratic and pluralistic society. Based upon the requirements for living in a multicultural, participatory democracy, the suggestions set forth in the remaining chapters of this book encompass an educational agenda that is similar to that outlined by Shapiro (1990). This agenda includes promoting a literacy that is consciously moral and political, one "that insists on the need to take sides—for social justice, human dignity, and the compassionate community—and provides the critical cultural skills through which society's real embodiment of these values can be assessed" (p. 25). It also involves teaching literacy in ways that empower students, in order to promote the "radical democratic restructuring of American life" (p. 25).

I argue that a literacy that is consciously moral and political is one that acknowledges the nonneutrality of language and texts. It is a literacy that welcomes interrogation and controversy, recognizing that it is only by wrestling with our differences that we will ever reach a common understanding. It is a literacy that acknowledges class struggle, racial unrest, and the continuation of oppression, and that seeks actively to eliminate social injustice through instructional practice. It is a literacy that promotes democratic participation and civic responsibility through consciously advancing the goal of equity. Finally, it is a literacy that cultivates a culture of compassion, that is, one that enhances students' capacity to care for others and for themselves (Noddings 1992, 1995).

A radical democratic restructuring will involve a redefinition of the canon, from one that is limited and elitist, to one that is all-encompassing—a story that is always in the process of being remade, a text that is continually being reshaped based upon the changing identity of our national community (Barber 1992). Thus, teaching literacy for empowerment must provide space for all voices to be heard so that all might contribute to the ongoing human narrative. Beyond this, however, it must also be a literacy that is enabling—one that gives every student the linguistic competence to participate equally in the remaking of American culture. Students must be led to a level of social consciousness whereby they see themselves as an integral part of the human society and recognize that, as members of that society, they have an obligation to interrogate the cultural values and beliefs that constitute it.

## TAKING SIDES: TOWARD A DEMOCRATIC COMMUNITY

An important argument that has been made for democratizing schools is that students must be actively engaged in the democratic process so that they might come to understand the nature of democratic life and be prepared for self-governance. Over eighty years ago, John Dewey argued that schools ought to function as democratic, participatory institutions, with democratic (versus merely economic) ideals as their goals, so that students would be led to internalize democratic processes and values. Dewey viewed democracy as a form of associated living, as the very idea of community life itself (Dewey 1916), and argued that students will only be able to understand what it means to live in a democratic society if schools themselves become microcosms of democracy (Detlefsen 1998; Stevens and Wood 1992). More recently, Amy Gutmann (1987) has suggested that the primary goal of education ought to be "the development of deliberative character that is essential to realizing the ideal of a democratically sovereign society" (p. 52). Barber (1984) writes that "The politically edifying influence of participation has been noted a thousand times since first Rousseau and then Mill and de Tocqueville suggested that democracy was best taught by practicing it" (p. 235). Other educational theorists have offered similar arguments for promoting democratic aims and for expanding the opportunities for democratic participation in schools (e.g., Callan 1993; Kaye and Curtis 1993; Gathercoal 1993; Wood 1988).

In the pages that follow, I argue that literacy instruction can make a vital contribution in preparing students for democratic participation. *Democracy,* however, is construed in a variety of ways; there is no singular, definitive definition of the term. Therefore, to avoid ambivalence, it is prudent to set forth a particular vision of democracy upon which the subsequent discussion of literacy is based. Admittedly, this discussion is cursory; readers who wish to pursue the topic further are invited to examine the complete works of the political and educational theorists cited herein.

Modern notions of democracy invoke visions of going to the polls and exercising our right to vote for the candidate that best represents our views. The theory of liberal democracy upon which our representative system of governance is based emerges from "premises about human nature, knowledge, and politics that are genuinely liberal but that are not intrinsically democratic" (Barber 1984, p. 4). This form of democracy—what Benjamin Barber (1984) refers to as "thin" democracy—is based upon the protection of property and private interests through limiting the role of government (hence the idea of "protectionist democracy").

Thin or protectionist democracy emerges from a long-standing fear of and distrust in popular rule. "An extensive and relatively ancient literature," writes Barber, "is devoted to the defense of politics against too much democracy and to the defense of democracy against too much participation. Every critique of majoritarianism, every critique of public opinion, every critique of mass politics conceals a deep distrust of popular participation" (1984, p. 8). Indeed, even Plato was said to be leery of governance by the general populace, preferring rule by an elite group of "philosopher kings" who were thought to have access to "the truth" (Arblaster 1987; Snauwaert 1993; Spring 1994).

Grounded in classical liberalism, contemporary Western democracy exalts the self-determination and autonomy of individuals. Political units and social conditions are arranged for the protection and preservation of individual rights and for the advancement of individual interests. This perspective, conceived by our forefathers as an antidote to traditional aristocracy and political repression, equates self-interest with the general good and freedom with the pursuit of individual happiness. According to Beyer and Liston (1996), classical liberal theory acknowledges the natural emergence of a dominant class:

> In the United States, the political and educational implications of [a classical liberal] view were clear as early as the writings of Thomas Jefferson, who presumed a "natural aristocracy" based on virtue and talents. . . . Within the economic sphere, the liberty that allows a natural aristocracy to rise to prominence is both inevitable and in the interest of all, as it maximizes personal well-being and the social good. (p. 50)

Barber (1992), too, notes our historical violation of democratic principles:

> America was at its founding not a notoriously democratic country. There was considerable suspicion of democracy, even bristling hostility against it; for democracy was feared as the rule of a propertyless rabble that would bring private prejudice and impassioned interests into the judicious deliberations of government. (p. 69)

Indeed, as Beyer and Liston note, many educational theorists to this day warn against the promotion of equality in the strictest sense, that is, an equality that views all individuals to be of equal worth. Creating a level playing field, such theorists suggest, leads to centralized control and government intrusion into our private lives. In contrast, the classical liberal tradition espouses a limited role for government, one whose primary function is to protect the natural rights of individual citizens. Such a role can best be manifested through a representative form of governance:

> A representative government composed, ideally, of those "natural aristocrats" elected to protect our individual interests is best suited to such a society. . . . The democratic state contained within this orientation, while providing a crucial shift away from older forms of aristocracy associated with inherited status, is thus rather limited. It allows the general population . . . to elect people to office who will protect their interests. And all governmental activity would be restricted to a fairly narrow sphere, surrounded by productive life within a market economy—but an economy, as we have seen, that could hardly be called democratic or geared toward advancing the interests of the common good. (p. 83)

For our purposes, it is important to differentiate between what might be considered a pure or ideal form of democracy, that is to say, a form of governance whereby there is equal political power (and, by extension, relatively equal economic power), and a protectionist or representative form of democracy.[1] Barber (1984) argues that with a protectionist system of governance, freedom is essentially a facade: "Representation is incompatible with freedom because it delegates and thus alienates political will at the cost of genuine self-government and autonomy. . . . Men and women who are not directly responsible through common deliberation, common decision, and common action for the policies that determine their common lives are not really free at all" (pp. 145–46). That is, with a thin or representative form of government, the primary responsibility for the preservation of individual rights, and for the expression of particular beliefs and values in political and economic policy, rests with a ruling elite. Hence, there is little *shared* authority.

Thin or protectionist democracy can be contrasted with direct or strong democracy in which every citizen participates in the creation of a civic community. In his book by the same name, Barber (1984) defines "strong democracy" as

> politics in the participatory mode where conflict is resolved in the absence of an independent ground through a participatory process of ongoing, proximate self-legislation and the creation of a political community capable of transforming dependent, private individuals into free citizens and partial and private interests into public goods. (p. 132)

A key concept in the definition of strong democracy is the notion of active participation in the formation of a civic community. Like Dewey, Barber regards democracy not merely as a product, but also as a *process*—one that maximizes public participation and involves resolving conflicts and arriving at decisions through open dialogue and debate. Democracy, in this sense, also implies a continuous examination and reformation of the common good through extensive and inclusive popular discussion.

It is also important to point out that embedded within the concept of participatory democracy are certain moral values, values that acknowledge the centrality of community and the worth of every individual. Strong democracy is, in the words of Barber (1992), an "aristocracy of everyone"—a society in which all persons are accorded the power to contribute to the decision-making process and the opportunity to share their perspectives in public forums. Hence, strong democracy endorses equality and justice and the transformation of society toward the realization of those ends. This perspective is articulated by Giroux (1993), who defines democracy as

> both a discourse and a practice that produces particular narratives and identities in-the-making informed by the principles of freedom, equality, and social justice. . . . When wedded to its most emancipatory possibilities, democracy encourages all citizens to actively construct and share power over those institutions that govern their lives. (p. 13)

While strong democracy is undoubtedly an unrealizable goal for large political structures such as the United States (the larger the society or institution, the more cumbersome direct participation becomes), it nevertheless can be endorsed on a smaller scale, for example within individual schools, workplaces, and even communities.[2] Such participation affords citizens more direct control over their lives and provides them with more decision-making power in those institutions and communities within which they live and work. A further argument for working toward a strong democratic system, as I suggest throughout this book, is that the democratic ideal embodies values to which we ought to aspire—values of freedom, equality, and social justice that, as Giroux has stated, can continue to shape our identity as a society. Yet, even within smaller structures such as committees, boards, and councils, true democratic participation is rare. That is, even in forums where citizens are provided a voice, there are often power differentials and hidden agendas that prohibit a serious consideration of alternative views. Consequently, individuals often leave feeling disempowered and alienated from the decision-making process—with a sense that they were not really *listened to*—rather than feeling empowered and affirmed.

To illustrate this point, let us consider school-based councils, which have been established in some states to promote greater community participation. Such councils can be highly effective when all constituencies are represented (for example, parents, teachers, students, and administrators) and, more importantly, when committee members are committed to engaging in open dialogue. What often occurs, however, is that some members may remain impervious to all perspectives but their own and may use power or influence to manipulate others into endorsing a particular view. Hence, as Bridges (1988) suggests, such discussions are not truly open, nor are they truly democratic, although they may appear to be so. It is also not unusual for members to spend an entire evening examining a particular issue, only to have an administrator exert his or her authority in making the final decision.

One might argue that such examples provide evidence that strong participatory governance simply will not work, even on a small scale. As a counterargument, however, it is important to recognize that, as a society, we have never taken seriously the need to prepare students for democratic participation. Rarely do we require students (or even teachers) to engage in constructive dialogue to solve problems or make decisions; rather, we generally resort to voting (a compromise, at best), or—even worse—to utilizing our authority as teachers or administrators in reaching a resolution. Indeed, it is even unusual for students to be given a genuine voice in school governance, beyond the limited advisory role of the student council.

What is striking in all of these scenarios are the ways in which differences in power and privilege become evident in discourse practices within the educational institution. To reiterate points made in previous chapters, classroom discussions often become reduced to attempts to discover what the teacher wants to hear, rather than being genuinely open forums where there is a true exchange of information and ideas. Such recitation patterns tend to marginalize and even silence students' voices, and those without the requisite cultural capital are even further removed from engaging in productive dialogue. What I am suggesting here is that literacy and language instruction in schools has often failed to provide students with the communicative competence required for true democratic participation—competence that requires students to listen, to be responsive to various points of view, to contribute their ideas, and to be willing to modify or even abandon their opinions when it seems warranted. In the next section, I examine ways to develop this competence.

## LITERACY FOR A PARTICIPATORY DEMOCRACY

To prepare students for civic action within a pluralistic society and to enhance the realization of a strong, participatory democracy, I argue that literacy and language instruction ought to be potentially transformative. That is, what is needed is a critical, proper literacy, one that helps students to see the transformative potential of language and that empowers them to become critical agents within a disparate and stratified society. What follows is an attempt to characterize literacy and language instruction that is informed by democratic principles and practices. I begin by proposing five basic criteria for examining literacy programs in our schools and classrooms, and then proceed by exploring how these criteria might be realized in practice. The first criterion is examined in the pages that follow; the remaining criteria are considered in the next two chapters. These criteria are not intended to be limiting or exclusive, but rather are meant to serve as a framework for examining pedagogical decisions. It is also important to point out that the boundaries delimiting these criteria are artificial ones, created only to facilitate discussion.

1. Literacy instruction ought to promote freedom of thought through encouraging diverse perspectives and welcoming productive critique.
2. Literacy instruction ought to enhance students' communicative competence by considering the social, cultural, and hegemonic dimensions of language use.
3. Literacy instruction ought to be consciously political.
4. Literacy ought to be taught in ways that make students aware of the power of language for transformation.
5. Literacy ought to be taught in ways that nurture a culture of compassion and care.

## Criterion No. 1: Literacy Instruction Ought to Promote Freedom of Thought through Encouraging Diverse Perspectives and Welcoming Productive Critique

In this section, I present two ways to accomplish this goal in schools. First, I examine open discussion or dialogue as a means for promoting freedom of thought by endorsing the free exchange of ideas. Second, I consider how the use of multiple texts, including multicultural and multiethnic texts, can further enhance freedom of thought by challenging students to consider diverse points of view.

### Encouraging Diverse Perspectives through Dialogue

Dialogue is an essential skill in a democratic society. Future citizens must be prepared to converse with one another through both spoken and written language, to share ideas and insights, to engage in genuine debate, and to modify their perspectives when warranted. Yet the dialogue that is generally promoted in classrooms does little to prepare students for democratic participation. Research shows that talk in classrooms is excessively teacher-centered, and students are given few opportunities for engaging in real discussion. For instance, in his comprehensive study of American education, Goodlad (1984) found that less than 1 percent of the time spent in classrooms required some type of open response from students; most of the talk in classrooms consisted of teacher monologue.

In his book entitled *Education, Democracy and Discussion* (1988), David Bridges argues persuasively that what is often seen as discussion is, in reality, an attempt by some individuals (e.g., the teacher, members of a committee, etc.) to coerce others into arriving at a single, proper conclusion. Such discussions, for example, are evident in ritualized patterns of classroom discourse mentioned in the previous chapter, for example, text reproduction patterns noted by D. Bloome (1987), and recitation patterns noted by Tharp and Gallimore (1991). The intent of these discourse patterns is to transmit information or to test students' existing knowledge—a form of banking education—rather than to promote critical reflection and to generate new knowledge. In contrast, to enter into a true discussion, suggests Bridges,

> is to be disposed to understand, to examine and to "take", or be affected by, opinions other than one's own. Furthermore I think one can claim that discussion would have no point unless there was reason to suppose that in general people's understanding or opinion was in fact modified by the consideration of alternative perspectives. (p. 16)

The primary intent of discussion, then, is the presentation of diverse perspectives. Hence, discussion also requires that all members of the community have a voice. Indeed, Bridges suggests that a necessary characteristic of discussion is the active engagement of all participants. This conceptualization of discussion is similar to that posed by critical theorists such as Paulo Freire, Donaldo Macedo, and Ira Shor, who argue for the centrality of dialogue in democratic and liberatory classrooms. These theorists are careful to distinguish between dialogue and monologue: A dialogue involves active engagement by more than one individual; a monologue does not (Boal 1996). Freire (1970/1993) writes that

> Dialogue is the encounter between men, mediated by the world, in order to name the world. Hence, dialogue cannot occur between those who want to name the world and those who do not wish this naming—between those who deny others the right to speak their word and those whose right to speak has been denied them. (p. 69)

Elsewhere, Freire states that

> Dialogue is a moment where humans meet to reflect on their reality as they make and remake it. . . . Dialogue is the sealing together of the teacher and the students in the joint act of knowing and re-knowing the object of study. (Shor and Freire 1987, pp. 98, 100)

Inherent in a definition of discussion or dialogue are the notions of open-mindedness and the reciprocal exchange of ideas. Such discussions are intentionally nonneutral in that students' cultural knowledge is sought as a primary source for deliberation and negotiation.

In examining the idea of dialogue, Shor (1992, pp. 94–96) contrasts two different styles of teacher talk: talk that is characteristically undemocratic in that it tends to silence students, and talk that is characteristically democratic in that it promotes dialogue. He describes an antidialogic discourse style as talk that uses academic or technical jargon; that asks questions requiring only brief, predetermined responses; that restricts time for thoughts and questions from students; that restricts discussion of students' experiences; that gives safe answers to students' questions; that limits discussion and writing to teacher-selected themes and readings; that discourages students from responding to the remarks of their peers; that discounts students' reactions when they stray from the information being sought by the teacher; that sends messages to students that they speak an inferior dialect; and that fails to acknowledge and accommodate the needs of women, persons of color, and others. A dialogic discourse, on the other hand, is talk that engages students in analysis; that avoids intimidating jargon; that poses thought-provoking, open-ended questions, and that encourages students to come up with their own questions for discussion; that gives students time to read, write, and reflect; that invites students to speak from their own experiences; that allows students to suggest themes of study; that encourages students to respond to the ideas of their peers; that respects students' nonstandard language as legitimate; that considers the needs of women, persons of color, and others by seeking equal participation and including culturally diverse curriculum; and that invites alternative interpretations of the topic under study.

Perhaps an illustration might be in order here. In my own teaching, students read a common chapter or article and reflect in personal journals prior to coming to class. (Occasionally, the reading and reflection takes place in class.) They are also asked to develop their own questions for class discussion. A typical class period begins with a brief review of the basic concepts in the reading, followed by large and small group dialogue that emerges from students' ideas, questions, and concerns. I do not have a preconceived agenda or list of outcomes; rather, the issues addressed are those that are central to the students in the class. A democratic dialogue might begin with any reading, video, photograph, or the like, followed by an open-ended question designed to elicit student response. The main feature that distinguishes open discussion from discourse that is nondemocratic is the amount of control students have over the learning process.

In contrast to dialogic instruction, research shows that most classrooms silence the voices of students by promoting antidialogic talk. Bridges (1988) states that discussion in schools and classrooms will be prohibited when the following conditions prevail:

—students are afraid (e.g. through fear of ridicule or reprisal) to speak freely;
—teachers do not think that pupils' opinions are worth listening to;
—people constantly interrupt or shout above expression of opinions they dislike;

—members of the group feel for some reason that it would be improper for
them to express a personal opinion;
—people are unamenable to the influence of reasons, evidence or argument.
(p. 25)

Nevertheless, as Bridges argues (and I concur), these are precisely the conditions that are present in many classrooms (as well as in many boardrooms).[3]

Discussion in schools is also prohibited when students are simply *not per-
mitted* to speak. This situation often results from an attempt by teachers to
control student behavior and reduce conflict through maintaining control of
classroom discourse. As McNeil's (1988) research reveals, limiting student
talk is a common practice in secondary schools, often stemming from the in-
security of teachers about allowing alternative views to be aired. As I suggest
in chapter three, a primary barrier to open dialogue is a lack of mutual trust
between teacher and learner. Yet antidialogic discourse tends to distance students and teachers, thereby further undermining the development of trusting
relationships that are necessary for democratic participation (Shor 1992).
Genuine discussion—one where all perspectives are affirmed and validated—
requires an environment that cultivates acceptance and that encourages both
students and teachers to take risks.

What is also required for genuine discussion to occur is a commitment to
open dialogue, that is, a willingness to share and to consider seriously differing views and perspectives. While this criteria may appear readily attainable,
in actuality it is very difficult to achieve, for teachers must be willing to surrender their authority and be amenable to positions that might vary greatly
from their own. That is, in free discussion, the teacher's voice becomes only
one of many.[4] Freire (1970/1993) states that true dialogue requires humility
on the part of both teachers and students:

> How can I dialogue if I always project ignorance onto others and never perceive
> my own? How can I dialogue if I regard myself as a case apart from others—mere
> "its" in whom I cannot recognize other "I"'s? How can I dialogue if I consider
> myself a member of the in-group of "pure" men, the owners of truth and knowl-
> edge, for whom all non-members are "these people" or "the great unwashed"?
> How can I dialogue if I start from the premise that naming the world is the task
> of an elite and that the presence of the people in history is a sign of deterioration,
> thus to be avoided? How can I dialogue if I am closed to—and even offended
> by—the contribution of others? How can I dialogue if I am afraid of being dis-
> placed, the mere possibility causing me torment and weakness? (p. 71)

Admittedly, a willingness to share authority with students is a difficult tran-
sition for many teachers, who are often reluctant to relinquish control. Nevertheless, for a discussion to be truly open, the role of the teacher must shift
from expert to moderator; that is, the teacher must create the conditions for

allowing free debate to occur. Students, too, must be willing to relinquish the passive role that is a typical result of more traditional pedagogy and accept the invitation to engage in collaborative inquiry. For students who have been conditioned to schooled literacy and to receiving the knowledge of others, they may resist genuine dialogue that requires active participation.

In contrast to being a transmitter of knowledge, the teacher's primary job in dialogic education becomes one of mediating the discussion so that productive communication can occur. Hence, the teacher must assure that no students dominate the exchange and that certain regulatory conventions are being adhered to so that productive communication can occur. It is important to acknowledge that promoting equality often involves creating conditions whereby the less powerful can speak, which sometimes necessitates constraining those who tend to be more verbal. The teacher's role, however, need not be solely a passive one. Rather, it can involve asking questions that extend student thinking; encouraging students to explore contradictions; clarifying students' ideas; and sharing alternate perspectives that challenge students' taken-for-granted assumptions. The primary consideration is that the teacher's voice should never dominate the process of mutual inquiry. Shor states that "Balancing the teacher's authority and the students' input is the key to making the process [of open dialogue] both critical and democratic" (1992, p. 85).

It is also important to note that, in a discussion that is truly open, there are no predetermined or prespecified learning outcomes or conclusions. Indeed, individuals within the group may arrive at very different conclusions, all of which may be rationally acceptable. In an era of outcomes-based education and educational accountability, such notions are quite radical. Teachers who value open discussion must be committed to free thought and the free exchange of ideas, without feeling unnecessarily bound by constraints to cover the state-mandated curriculum. Such teachers must also be committed to creating a public forum where all opinions can be shared, even those that may be discomfiting to others in the class, for example, racial prejudice, gender bias, and so on. While such free exchange can lead to conflict, within the confines of a classroom it can also open the way to honest debate. Barber (1992) makes a convincing argument when he states that

> You do not improve the educational climate for challenging bigotry or respond to those it injures by suspending or expelling violators . . . for they are precisely those most in need of education. When bigotry appears in the classroom, the issues are pedagogical, not legal, and remedies must be instructive rather than punitive. Schools are neither courtrooms nor prisons where the guilty are prosecuted and punished. They are workshops for overcoming prejudice; we would scarcely need them if they enrolled only the tolerant and the just. (p. 97)

Teaching tolerance—which is a limited response to cultural difference at best—ought to be an uncontested goal of educational institutions within a pluralistic, democratic society. By ignoring bigotry and more subtle forms of personal prejudice, we merely perpetuate these attitudes through our silence.

Perhaps an even greater obstacle to genuine dialogue is that those who are engaged in open discussion must be receptive to discovering hidden biases, presuppositions, and misinterpretations. Bridges writes that "In the type of discussion I am here defining, members of a group will be especially wary of the possibility that their pursuit of insight, understanding, knowledge or a solution to a problem will be inhibited by their own unexamined (even unrecognized) prejudice and assumptions" (p. 70). That is, we must be willing to acknowledge that, "as right as we truly know ourselves to be, there is that sliver of a possibility that we may be wrong" (Paterson 1992, p. 55). Open discussion can help us to understand that our knowledge of the world is only partial—indeed, that knowing itself must always be viewed as partial and incomplete (Ellsworth 1989).

Genuine dialogue can also help students and teachers work through the multiple expressions that emerge from sometimes competing subjectivities as men, women, members of a particular social class, and members of a particular race or ethnic group. Our individual worlds are multifaceted and complex; we do not speak with a single voice but rather with several, sometimes contradictory, voices.[5] Knoblauch and Brannon (1993) write that "Any classroom is a site of conflicting beliefs, values, affiliations, desires, class and gender identities, the tapping of which can offer opportunity for critical reflection" (p. 65).

Herein lies the value of discussion in a pluralistic, democratic society, for through examining the perspectives of others, our own taken-for-granted assumptions are challenged and made visible. Understanding that our perspectives are incomplete and sometimes contradictory can be a humbling experience; at the same time, it can make us more receptive to alternate perspectives and more accepting of different ways of seeing the world. It is through such discussions that we come to understand and appreciate views that differ from our own; however, it is important to note that open expression requires a disposition on the part of those engaged in the discussion to listen to alternative views and a willingness to alter their own beliefs when warranted. The development of this disposition among both students and teachers often will require time, forbearance, and a steadfast commitment to open dialogue.

Clearly, not all learning can occur in this fashion. Nevertheless, it can be argued that whenever possible, dialogue ought to be the preferred method of learning, for it provides for democratic deliberation—a mode of decision making that is required for the evolution of a truly democratic society. Through discussion, there is a sense of shared power: all voices are acknowledged, all cultural knowledge is legitimated. Open discussion also enhances the development of a shared community, for "It requires social involvement, co-operation, mutual attentiveness and responsiveness, respect and appreciation of individual divergence, reasonableness, etc.—the kind of qualities and relations which, one might argue, lie at the heart of democratic community" (Bridges 1988, p. 130). Hence, open discussion can contribute to the development of civic virtue through providing experiences for reciprocal relationships and constructive debate within a community of learning.

### Encouraging Diverse Perspectives through Using Multiple Texts

Another way that power can be equalized and shared in classrooms is through the use of multiple and diverse texts. To prepare students for democratic participation in a pluralistic society, our choice of texts must be inclusionary; that is, texts must be selected that incorporate perspectives from groups that have traditionally been marginalized or even silenced. Students must be able to see themselves in the texts we use in our classrooms—a point I take up in greater detail in a later chapter. That is, their lives must be validated through the materials that we use; they must come to understand the significance of their voices within a democratic society. At the same time, however, using texts that incorporate multicultural identities and that include diverse points of view can challenge our assumptions, expand our horizons, and introduce us to different ways of perceiving the world.

As I argue above, textbooks tend to be largely Eurocentric; that is, a White, primarily male, and middle-class worldview is endorsed through a practice of mentioning the contributions of nonmainstream populations (versus discussing them in any depth) and through the desire of publishing companies to omit potentially controversial topics. Further, recent research shows that the literature selections used in high schools and colleges continue to be exclusionary, and the classical Western literary canon remains largely uncontested. Citing research by the Modern Language Association, Graff (1992) notes that the college literary canon remains essentially unchanged except for "accretion at the margins" (p. 24). Applebee's research in high school classrooms presents an equally dismal picture (Applebee 1989, 1991).[6]

In addition to these visible marginalizing practices, censorship of alternate perspectives often occurs in more subtle ways. For instance, research shows that books that are recommended for children often promote an individualistic versus collectivist ideology, that is, one of personal self-development and self-reliance versus group responsibility and collaborative response (Shannon 1992). It is worth noting that this ideology, which is deeply embedded in Western thought (Bellah, Madsen, Sullivan, Swidler, and Tipton 1985), has been found to have a particular detrimental effect on high-achieving nonmainstream students, who tend to internalize a model of self-sufficiency and self-reliance and subsequently reject needed support from their peers—a decision that is often "disastrous for academic achievement" (Fordham 1991, p. 91).

Our role as educators is to educate, not indoctrinate. Teaching from any singular, ethnocentric persuasion limits our students' abilities to perceive issues and concepts from other perspectives, to think critically, to consider various points of view. Thus, expanding the canon requires that we provide a multiplicity of perspectives—perspectives provided by Native Americans, African Americans, Asian Americans, Caribbean Americans, Mexican Americans, Hispanics/Latinos, and individuals from other nations, as well as Europeans; perspectives of both women and men; perspectives of those who embrace alternative ideologies; and perspectives that are representative of other forms of human otherness. James Banks (1994) writes:

> Only a curriculum that reflects the experiences of a wide range of groups in the United States and the world, and the interests of those groups, is in the national interest and is consistent with the public good. Any other kind of curriculum reflects a special interest and is inconsistent with the needs of a nation that must survive in a pluralistic and highly interdependent world. (p. 23)

Banks argues that to have a truly integrated curriculum, we must experience a shift in paradigms. That is, the basic structure of the curriculum must change to incorporate diverse voices and multiple perspectives. Thus, a study of the western European advancement would involve readings and discussions that challenge students' taken-for-granted assumptions about the Westward Movement ("West" according to whom?) and that explore this historical era from the Native American perspective. A study of the establishment of the American West would include examining the experiences of Irish and Chinese immigrants, many of whom lost their lives constructing the transcontinental railway system. A study of World War II would involve an examination of the internment of Japanese Americans living in the United States (Takaki 1993). Typical approaches to multicultural education that focus on heroes and holidays (the contributions approach) or that merely add content to an already established curriculum (the additive approach), do little to challenge the prevailing canon. In fact, Banks points out that "most of the ethnic groups and women added to the curriculum have values and roles consistent with those of the dominant culture"; those who challenged the status quo "are less likely to be selected for inclusion into the curriculum" (1994, p. 26).

To assure that diverse perspectives are included, teachers will need to enhance the curriculum through readings, editorials, speeches, videos, and other media sources that challenge the assumptions stated in the required text(s). Field trips and interviews with persons in the community (e.g., Vietnam veterans, senior citizens, Native Americans, migrant farm workers, corporate executives, etc.) also provide rich learning possibilities. Students can be encouraged to conduct research on various topics, write essays and narratives from alternative points of view, role play moments in history, and debate controversial issues. The challenge is to engage students in ideological conflict by incorporating texts and learning experiences that provide opportunities for critique.

Another way of challenging and expanding students' perspectives is through incorporating multicultural and multiethnic literature throughout the curriculum. Spears-Bunton (1998) writes of the value of incorporating multicultural perspectives through literature:

> Multicultural-literature experiences instill the disposition in communities of readers to weigh new knowledge against old knowledge, taken-for-granted assumptions and to question the attitudes and behaviors that accompany reified knowledge. Multicultural-literature experiences situate readers to respectfully consider (and reconsider) the world views and human exigencies of others. A multicultural perspective labels no part of humanity as trivial; it unsilences humanity's voices, and it seeks and welcomes opportunities to include and honor diverse cultural ways of creating knowledge and metaphorical ways of understanding. (pp. 20–21)

Multicultural texts have become abundant in recent years, and it is not difficult to find books that "unsilence humanity's voices." For instance, Laurence Yep's *Dragon's Gate* chronicles the dangers faced by Chinese immigrants as they constructed the transcontinental railroad, and Clifford Trafzer's *California's Indians and the Gold Rush* examines the role of Native Americans in the mining of gold in California. Both could be used in conjunction with a study of western advancement and development. Study of World War II could include the reading of Yoshiko Uchida's *Desert Exile*, which describes her family's experiences with Japanese relocation during World War II. Barbara Cohen's *The Long Way Home* explores the impact on a family when their mother is diagnosed with cancer, and it could accompany a study of disease in a biology class. Numerous books can be used to augment the study of economics by exploring the human impact of poverty and homelessness. In fact, there are literally hundreds of multicultural and multiethnic children's books and young adult novels that can be used to enhance a variety of topics in history, science, and even mathematics classes.

A pluralized literary canon can also be used in language arts classes to examine a particular theme. For instance, a study of immigration might include texts by diverse authors that capture the experiences of various immigrant populations as they experience a new and often unwelcoming world; a theme of "Growing Up" might include books, poetry, and other readings that explore childhood experiences and expectations in diverse cultures. Oliver (1994) provides several examples of thematic units that can be used in classrooms, from "A Cross-Cultural Look at Who We Are" to "A Study of Values" (pp. 181–84). She suggests that readings for a unit entitled "We the Americans: Beginnings" might include Alex Haley's *Roots*, Maureen Crane Wartski's *A Boat to Nowhere*, Gregory Orfalea's *Before the Flames*, Rose Cohen's *Out of the Shadow*, Gro Svendsen's *Frontier Mother*, Marie Hall Ets's *Rosa*, Ignatia Broker's *Night Flying Woman*, Ole Rolvaag's *Giants in the*

*Earth,* E. L. Doctorow's *World's Fair,* Isaac Bashevis Singer's "Tanhum," and
the film *El Norte.* Another excellent resource for teaching thematically using
multicultural and multiethnic literature is Frances Ann Day's *Multicultural
Voices in Contemporary Literature* (1994), which lists associated themes for
each annotation and provides a comprehensive subject index.

Incorporating multicultural and multiethnic texts in the curriculum not
only provides students with diverse perspectives, but it also helps them learn
about prejudice, injustice, and the violence and hopelessness of oppression.
Arguing for the inclusion of multicultural literature, Oliver (1994) writes:

> Writers often reflect the environments in which they live, and many racial and eth-
> nic groups in this country face extremely oppressive environments. . . . Sometimes
> teachers tell me that their students would "really be upset" by much of the "eth-
> nic literature" that they have read. "It's so violent," they protest. "It's so stereo-
> typic," they complain. But should we shelter our mainstream, middle-class, roof-
> over-their-heads, full-stomach students? Shouldn't they know that a world other
> than their own exists? All too often, students live in a vacuum. (p. 125)

Reading multicultural and multiethnic literature will not always be pleasant,
but should it be? As Oliver points out, large numbers of our population must
face poverty, violence, and physical and emotional abuse on a daily basis. Admittedly, these are controversial issues. Yet these are issues that our students
must be prepared to confront; certainly, they will not be addressed through
our silence.

Thus far our discussion of democratic inclusion has focused on our human
differences; however, it is also important to point out that multicultural/mul-
tiethnic literature can help us to uncover our sameness. Literature is the stuff
of life; it elicits aesthetic and personal responses that connect us at a profoundly human level (Spears-Bunton 1990). What young student will not relate to the anguish of thirteen-year-old Jessie as he witnesses the horrors on a
slave ship in Paula Fox's *Slave Dancer*? Or to the anger of Josias as he is forced
to vacate a bus so that white folks can board in Mildred Taylor's *Mississippi
Bridge*? Or to the remorse of young Nathaniel, when he says:

> last year when Mama died
> I went to my room to hide
> from the hurt
> I closed my door
> wasn't going to come out
> no more, never
> but my uncle he said
>
> you going to get past
> this pain
>         you going to

push on past this pain
and one of these days
you going to feel like
yourself again

I don't miss a day
remembering Mama
sometimes I cry
but mostly
I think about
the good things
now
("Missing Mama"
in *Nathanial Talking*
by Eloise Greenfield [1988])

Good literature exposes our common identity; it touches us in ways that reveal our collective human experience. In essence, literature contains universal themes that speak to us all—themes that transcend our differences and help us to see the world through another's eyes.

## CONCLUSION

In this chapter, I argue that literacy instruction ought to reflect democratic aims—aims that embrace the values of equity, social justice, and responsible civic action that are required for the realization of a strong, participatory democracy. I suggest that democratic participation can be realized in classrooms by accommodating multiple perspectives through the use of genuine dialogue and through the incorporation of multicultural/multiethnic texts. It is important to point out that encouraging the free exchange of ideas does not exclude the Western European perspective; however, this perspective is regarded as only one of many and hence is not privileged above all others.

At the same time, we must acknowledge that a democratically structured classroom will not be embraced by everyone. Not all students (or teachers) will be receptive to open dialogue; not all students (or teachers) will be willing to consider alternate views. Further, a commitment to democratization requires that we must be willing to allow prejudicial attitudes to be voiced, and that we be sensitive to the ways in which some voices may be silenced.

Even in such circumstances, however, democratic discourse can be productive. Oliver (1994) describes a student named "Jerry" who "wouldn't budge on any issue," whose narrow-mindedness continued despite her best efforts. Yet, Oliver also states that "I do believe . . . that Jerry's writing improved in my class. I also think that we changed his manner of expression by the time the semester was over; the disapproving responses he got from his classmates for his outbursts were not what he expected. If we didn't change his thinking, at least we altered his behavior somewhat by demonstrating that his was not the only voice that deserved to be heard" (p. 127).

Such is the nature of democratic participation. We may do little to alter students' basic beliefs (nor do we have the right to do so). Yet the presentation of multiple perspectives encourages students (and teachers) to see society from different vantage points, to confront their ethnocentric assumptions, and to respect alternate ways of viewing the world. Acknowledging that ours is "not the only voice that deserves to be heard" will do much toward realizing a democratic vision.

## NOTES

1. Democracy literally means rule by the many. In a pure democracy, no distinction is made between the ruler and the ruled; rather, each citizen is considered sovereign. Most would argue that a pure system of democratic governance is impossible except in situations where there is a relatively limited populace, such as the Greek city-state. (See Arblaster 1987; Snauwaert 1993.)

2. Barber (1984) calls such social constructions "mediating institutions" (p. 249) and suggests that these institutions can facilitate communication, thereby enhancing civic participation. He also suggests that increased communication made possible by technological advancements can help reduce "problems of scale" associated with national societies. To promote strong democracy, Barber calls for a national system of neighborhood assemblies that would provide forums for public discussion of local, regional, and national issues.

3. It is instructive to consider the ways in which the media reinforces erroneous notions of discussion. Daytime television talk shows have become extremely popular in recent years, yet generally the participants talk at one another rather than engage in genuine dialogue. Alternative perspectives are rarely accorded serious consideration or respect; indeed, it is not unusual for participants to resort to shouting, name calling, and other forms of castigation. The dialogue that is promoted could hardly be considered an effective model of democratic discourse for the general populace.

4. One might even argue that, in a truly open discussion, the teacher is obligated to withhold his or her point of view. Bridges (1988) writes that, where a teacher puts forth his opinions even "modestly," students find it difficult not to treat his opinions as "having special authority" (p. 120). He also suggests that students' ability to view the teacher's perspective as only one of many may be a developmental process. Hence, it may be necessary for the teacher to remain neutral until a climate of mutual trust and regard has been established.

5. In an often-cited critique of critical pedagogy, Ellsworth (1989) argues that "Dialogue in its conventional sense is impossible in the culture at large because at this historical moment, power relations between raced, classed, and gendered students and teachers are unjust. The injustice of these relations and the way in which those injustices distort communication cannot be overcome in a classroom, no matter how committed the teacher and students are to 'overcoming conditions that perpetuate suffer-

ing'" (p. 316). I do not believe her criticism is meant to imply that we should dismiss dialogue entirely as an avenue for learning; rather, it cautions that the teacher must be cognizant of the power structure within the classroom and the ways in which differentials in power can silence and distance both students and teachers.

6. I do not wish to suggest that we ought to eliminate the classics. Rather, what I am advocating is an expansion of the literary canon to include non-European literature and literature written by women. I concur with Pagano, when she writes that "I find my teaching of canonical works immeasurably enhanced when I put them in conversation with noncanonical works. . . . Similarly, noncanonical works become richer when they are located with respect to canonical traditions" (Pagano and Miller 1993, p. 150).

# 5

## Promoting a Critical Literacy

Initially, I resist the idea of the "oppressor's language," certain that this construct has the potential to disempower those of us who are just learning to speak, who are just learning to claim language as a place where we make ourselves subject. *"This is the oppressor's language yet I need it to talk to you."* Adrienne Rich's words. Then, when I first read these words, and now, they make me think of standard English, of learning to speak against black vernacular, against the ruptured and broken speech of a dispossessed and displaced people. Standard English is not the speech of exile. It is the language of conquest and domination; in the United States, it is the mask which hides the loss of so many tongues. . . .

To heal the splitting of mind and body, we marginalized and oppressed people attempt to recover ourselves and our experiences in language. We seek to make a place for intimacy. Unable to find such a place in standard English, we create the ruptured, broken, unruly speech of the vernacular. When I need to say words that do more than simply mirror or address the dominant reality, I speak black vernacular. There, in that location, we make English do what we want it to do. We take the oppressor's language and turn it against itself. We make our words a counter-hegemonic speech, liberating ourselves in language. (bell hooks, *Teaching to Transgress*, p. 168; pp. 174–75)

For far too many years, the oppressor's language has been the only acceptable language of schools and society. A common practice of teachers in some of the schools I have visited is to keep grammar slammers, fictional boxes where students are instructed to file their bad language with a warning that it never emerge again. The intent is to denounce, to degrade, and finally to destroy the remnants of group identity that are captured in their language—to render meaningless those ways of saying and being that differ from the linguistic norms of those who are in power. Yet we simultaneously require that students embrace the language of those who oppress them, that they accept as superior a language that has been used to silence them, that they deny their linguistic heritage—the language of their homes, families, communities—and learn to speak with an alien voice.

We silence students in many ways. We silence them through antidialogic practices that deny their experiences and encourage complacency. We silence them through marginalizing their histories, their struggles, their collective voices. We silence them through denigrating their language, denouncing their behaviors, and discrediting their cultural expressions. Finally, we silence them by teaching them that it is through their own inadequacies, their own ignorance, that they have failed.

An empowering literacy provides students with a counterhegemonic language. It is a language that teaches students how to resist by creating space for their own words to be voiced; that teaches them how speech works to empower and oppress; that teaches them the forms and structures of the language of power while celebrating their unique linguistic contributions. It is also a language that illuminates reality, that challenges students to interrogate their unexamined assumptions, and that encourages social responsibility and civic action. A critical literacy is one that liberates; a counterhegemonic language is one that takes sides—toward a more just, equitable, and compassionate world.

## CREATING A COUNTERHEGEMONIC DISCOURSE

The previous chapter presented ways for realizing a democratic discourse in classrooms. Establishing a dialogical classroom is an important requisite for realizing a critical literacy. To understand the transformative potential of language, students must believe that their voices will be heard and that their ideas will be legitimated. Merely creating conditions for genuine dialogue to occur, however, is not enough. For literacy to be potentially transformative, it must address the issues that divide us as a society. It must tread into unsafe, controversial territory. In other words, it must be consciously political. In this chapter, I explore two means for giving students a counterhegemonic discourse: first, through teaching them the social, cultural, and hegemonic functions of language while simultaneously helping them to master the language of power; and second, through providing experiences that will encourage students to develop a critical consciousness.

### Criterion No. 2: Literacy Instruction Ought to Enhance Students' Communicative Competence by Considering the Social, Cultural, and Hegemonic Dimensions of Language Use

In a pluralistic, democratic society, individuals must possess a range of communicative resources. We must be able to communicate with those who are considerably different from ourselves, to make our views known, and to understand the pragmatic functions of language. We must be able to use language for different purposes: to share ideas, to express opinions, to persuade others. We must also acquire knowledge about the hegemonic functions of language use so that we can come to understand the emancipatory potential of language. Hence, developing oral and written competence involves not only learning the discourse of power, but it also involves acquiring various secondary discourses so that we can learn how to communicate in a variety of social contexts.

Language use does not occur in a vacuum. The linguistic choices we make in particular social situations are dependent upon the "context of situation," that is, what is occurring, and the nature of the event in which the language is being used (field), the relationship of the participants (tenor), and the role that language plays in the social interchange (mode) (Halliday and Hasan 1985). The language used between a physician and patient in a doctor's office, for instance, will be very different from the language used between two lifelong friends at the local bar. Therefore, to teach language outside of its social context—through worksheets, textbook exercises, and so on—trivializes the teaching of language by divorcing its form from its pragmatic functions. What is needed is a conception of language as situated speech that is shaped by the context in which it is being used.

Beyond this, however, appropriate language use requires that we also express particular beliefs and attitudes associated with the context in which the language is being used (Gee 1989, 1990). That is, language use is not only social, it is also *cultural* in that it is acquired within particular communities— communities that share certain assumptions and rules used to govern appropriate linguistic behavior. To reiterate briefly the ideas presented in a previous chapter, individuals possess several discourses, and these discourses carry with them particular ways of being in the world. James Paul Gee (1990, p. 142) defines a discourse as "a sort of 'identity kit' which comes complete with the appropriate costume and instructions on how to act, talk, and often write, so as to take on a particular social role that others will recognize." To be initiated into a discourse, then, involves becoming knowledgeable about the ways of talking, acting, believing, dressing, and behaving that are associated with that discourse. Hence, the discourse of being a teacher requires particular ways of talking, acting, and behaving (along with the use of certain props) that are associated with teachers; the discourse of being a police officer requires particular ways of talking, acting, and behaving like police officers. Similarly, the discourse of school involves the acceptance of particular attitudes and beliefs associated with educational institutions. Membership in a particular social group or social network requires that individuals learn how to speak, act, and think like the other members of the group.

Gee (1990) makes an important distinction between *acquisition* and *learning* that is relevant to the present discussion. According to Gee, acquisition is essentially a subconscious process that involves "picking up" a group's language and social practices through the natural process of enculturation. Learning, on the other hand, is a conscious process that requires explicit instruction. Gee argues that discourses cannot be mastered through overt instruction; rather, they are *acquired* by interacting with persons who are already proficient in the discourse. "This is how we all acquired our native language and our home-based Discourse. It is how we acquire all later, more public oriented Discourses. If you have no access to the social practice, you don't get in the Discourse, you don't have it" (p. 147). Therefore, according to Gee, teaching a discourse through overt classroom instruction will not, in and of itself, enable students to master a discourse. Being able to talk about a discourse (describe it, define the rules for usage, etc.) does not mean that an individual will be able to actually use the discourse in social interaction. Rather, to teach students a secondary discourse, including the language of power, students must be "apprenticed"; that is, they must practice being a member of that particular social group through active participation in that group.[1] This notion has tremendous implications for developing young authors and readers and will be examined in greater depth in the next chapter. For our present purposes, let us examine further the implications of Gee's ideas for students' language development.

Gee claims that each of us has a primary discourse, the discourse into which we have been acculturated as part of our socialization within the family. In addition, we each have several secondary discourses that we acquire through participation in various social institutions, including schools, churches, clubs, workplaces, and so on. Classroom instruction serves an important function in that it can expose students to various secondary discourses, thereby expanding their communicative competence.[2] Effective literacy instruction, according to Gee, involves both learning and acquisition. Good teachers serve as apprentices, scaffolding students' growing ability to "say, do, value, believe, within that Discourse" (p. 154), through demonstrating their own mastery of the discourse and supporting the efforts of their students. That is, teaching in this sense requires that we model effective use of the discourse and that we provide opportunities for students to practice using the discourse through incorporating authentic, meaningful, real-life experiences. Good teachers also engage students in the process of learning by guiding them in an understanding of the forms and structures of language, so that they can acquire meta-level cognitive and linguistic knowledge.

While helping students to acquire secondary discourses is essential, equipping students with meta-knowledge about language through overt instruction is also important, for such knowledge can be used to critique and analyze language use. Gee argues that "Meta-knowledge is power, because it leads to the ability to manipulate, to analyze, to resist while advancing. Such meta-knowledge can make 'maladapted' students smarter than 'adapted' ones" (pp.

148–49). Thus, gaining knowledge about the "meta-elements" of language through learning a secondary discourse can be liberating, for it provides a means for evaluating and critiquing various discourses, including one's primary discourse. For nonmainstream students, learning a secondary discourse—such as the dominant, mainstream discourse—provides them with insights into the dominant discourse that those who have acquired this discourse through enculturation (i.e., as a primary discourse) do not have. For mainstream students who come to school having acquired the discourse of power, studying nonmainstream discourses can help them understand the complexity of other linguistic forms and thereby acquire meta-knowledge about their own discourse and the ways in which it functions to privilege and oppress. Hence, Gee suggests that "liberating literacy . . . almost always involves learning, and not just acquisition" (p. 154).

As a teacher of nonmainstream university students, Mike Rose provided his students with "access to the social practices" of the dominant academic discourse. Rose served as a literacy apprentice in that he modeled the process of inquiry for his students; at the same time, he also taught students the form and structure of academic prose. One compelling example cited in *Lives on the Boundary* (1989) involves Olga, an older student who had "the lines of a hard life across her forehead" (p. 161). Rose describes his work with Olga as he diligently strives to teach her the challenging plays of Shakespeare:

> I'd sit with her and drag her through a scene, paraphrasing a speech, summarizing a conflict. Sometimes I'd force her to direct her anger at the play, to talk at it, make her articulate exactly why she hated it, be as precise as she could about how it made her feel to sit here with this book. Finally, we finished *Macbeth*. One night in that eggshell basement lunchroom, she wrapped her hands around her cola and began to tap it on the table: "You know, Mike, people always hold this shit over you, make you . . . make you feel stupid with their fancy talk. But now *I've* read it, I've read Shakespeare, I can say I, *Olga*, have read it."

In her book *Other People's Children* (1995), Lisa Delpit documents another instance of linguistic apprenticeship. "Marge" had received a fellowship granted to increase the numbers of faculty holding doctorates at Black colleges, but she lacked the GRE scores determined necessary for doing acceptable doctoral-level work. She was subsequently accepted into a master's program, and "Susan," a faculty member at the institution, was assigned to work with her. Delpit describes their work together:

> Susan began a program to help Marge learn how to cope with the academic setting. Susan recognized early on that Marge was very talented but that she did not understand how to maneuver her way through academic writing, reading, and talking. In their first encounters, Susan and Marge discussed the comments instructors had written on Marge's papers, and how the next paper might incorporate the

professor's concerns. The next summer Susan had Marge write weekly synopses of articles related to educational issues. When they met, Marge talked through her ideas while Susan took notes. Together they translated the ideas into the "discourse of teacher education." Marge then rewrote the papers referring to their conversations and Susan's extensive written comments. (p. 156)

Delpit goes on to state that Marge mastered the dominant academic discourse and became a "real star" within the academy. Both of these situations, I believe, provide a good example of the apprentice-type relationship that is required to master a secondary discourse.

Perhaps the best illustration of instruction that applies Gee's principles of language learning can be found in June Jordan's descriptions of her classroom, cited at the beginning of this book. Working with primarily African American university students who had been conditioned to accept the myth of standard English as a superior linguistic form, Jordan (1988) guided her students in a comprehensive study of the rules and regularities of the Black vernacular. Through this process, her students came to understand the consistency and complexity of their primary discourse and thereby gained a respect for the language of their community. They also acquired important meta-knowledge concerning the ways in which language is viewed as cultural capital within a hierarchically ordered society, and an understanding of how language is used either to empower or to silence. Another important lesson to be gained from Jordan's classroom is that literacy can only be liberating if students' native languages, that is, their primary discourses, are valued and affirmed.

It might be argued, as Delpit (1995) does, that Gee's theory of language is overly deterministic in that mastery of any discourse involves a process of enculturation: "instead of being locked into 'your place' by your genes, you are now locked hopelessly into a lower-class status by your discourse" (p. 154).[3] While Delpit's concern is certainly a crucial one, I do not read Gee this way. As Gee suggests, we all have mastered a number of secondary discourses, albeit to varying degrees. (Consider, for example, that many of the readers of this book have undoubtedly mastered the discourse of teacher or professor, along with other secondary discourses.) Rather, I believe Gee presents a realistic portrayal of what is required in learning a secondary discourse—that students cannot master a discourse beyond their primary one solely through a focus on structure and form. That is, in addition to analyzing the structure of language, students also need to be immersed in the discourse they are attempting to master, whether it be a dominant discourse, a schooled discourse, or any number of discourses required within various secondary institutions. Such immersion can be provided by teachers who are committed to supporting students in their linguistic development—through providing a model of the discourse and scaffolding their use of the discourse as they attempt to gain mastery. It is precisely this form of apprenticeship that Mike Rose provided in his work with Olga, and that Susan provided in her work with Marge.

Linda Christensen, a high school teacher in Portland, Oregon, also provides this type of apprenticeship (Christensen 1994). Christensen helps her students become proficient in the standard discourse (what she refers to as the "cash language") by teaching them the rules of the language while simultaneously giving them meta-information about language use. Her students make up tests that Standard English speakers would find difficult; they read articles, stories, and poems written in Standard English and compare them with those written in nonstandard dialects; they analyze the spoken discourse found on videotapes. Christensen reports that most of her students "like the sound of their home language better. They like the energy, the poetry, and the rhythm of the language" (p. 145). At the same time, they talk about why it is necessary to learn Standard English by determining "who makes the rules, who benefits from the rules, who loses from the rules, who uses the rules to keep some in and keep others out."

Helping students acquire a secondary discourse through immersion in that discourse can also be done through role play, discussion, and critique. For instance, students might learn the standard discourse by role playing a conversation with the superintendent; by practicing formal oral presentations; by giving persuasive speeches to their peers; by performing a mock television talk show; by conducting interviews with persons from the community; by analyzing famous speeches. Students can also learn the discourse of power by writing for authentic purposes and audiences: letters to the editor, pamphlets and brochures that are distributed in the community, student-produced books and magazines. To acquire a secondary discourse, students must be immersed in meaningful, purposeful language use within authentic social contexts.

Providing students with meaningful and authentic opportunities to use oral and written language, however, is not enough. We must also be honest with our students about the hegemonic function of language, so that acquiring a secondary discourse is a choice, and not an imposition. To be more specific, teaching students how dominant discourses function as gatekeepers in our society—that is, illuminating the beliefs and attitudes associated with dominant discourses—allows students to reject those beliefs and attitudes (the dominant identity) while simultaneously acquiring competence in using the language of power. Students can learn how to take on a particular social role that others will recognize by using the appropriate costumes and instructions on how to act, talk, and often write without embracing the value system inherent in the discourse. Hence, both mainstream and nonmainstream students are able to make a conscious decision as to whether they want to join the dominant discourse club.

At the same time, we must validate students' primary discourses by celebrating their linguistic expressions. We affirm their language, for instance, when we make their cultural experiences and personal passions a primary source of classroom writing (Blake 1997; Bomer 1995; Calkins 1986/1994; Calkins and Harwayne 1991; Graves 1994), when we ask students to bring in tape-recorded stories from their families, when we invite them to interview senior citizens in their neighborhoods, when we examine the uses of non-standard dialects in storybooks and novels, and when we study the effectiveness of their primary discourses in various social contexts. Students ought to be encouraged to play with language, to share interesting uses of their primary discourse, and to practice effective ways of integrating their own primary linguistic form with texts that use the standard form.

Students' language is also affirmed when we focus on their ideas in their oral and written texts, rather than on form. Christensen makes an essential point when she states that "When more attention is paid to the way something is written or said than to what is said, students' words and thoughts become devalued. Students learn to be silent, to give as few words as possible for teacher criticism" (1994, p. 143). Certainly, learning about the superficial features of language (spelling, mechanics, grammatical structure, etc.) is not inconsequential; however, as writing educators will remind us, dealing with form ought to come after we have celebrated students' thoughts and experiences. We give students a voice when we value both what they say and how they say it; we empower them when we teach them how to read the world.

### Criterion No. 3: Literacy Instruction Ought to Be Consciously Political

In our discussion thus far, we have examined language as both a social and a cultural system. Language use varies according to the social context in which it is used; it also serves as an identity kit that defines our membership in particular cultural groups. Teaching students about the hegemonic function of language is one way of helping them to read the world by making literacy instruction consciously political. I have suggested that a study of language difference ought to be an integral part of the language arts program, so that students are led to challenge the privileged status of the standard discourse and to appreciate the complexity and richness of our diverse linguistic heritage. I have also suggested that students need to be provided opportunities to learn language in authentic social contexts, so that they might develop the communicative competence necessary for participating in diverse institutions and with diverse others within a democratic society. We have also examined the notion of discussion in some depth as yet another way to use language in classrooms. Open discussion or dialogue has been presented as a means for sharing power through the process of mutual inquiry and deliberation; thus it serves to initiate students into the requirements needed for democratic participation.

In this section I argue that, in addition to these pedagogical opportunities, we must provide learning experiences for our students that help them to uncover their cultural assumptions and develop a critical consciousness. I suggest that our instruction ought to be consciously political; that is, we ought to teach in ways that illuminate reality and that encourage students to enter into critical dialogue, so that they might become educated to make informed moral and civic decisions. More specifically, we must provide students with a "counterdiscourse" (Simon 1992) that would enable them to discover, name, and potentially seek to change oppressive conditions in society.

The choices we make as teachers are never value-free. The decision to use a particular instructional program or to follow a particular textbook, the decision to provide for collaborative inquiry, the decision to utilize a particular computer software program—all of these decisions are grounded in an ideological stance concerning what knowledge is most important and whose knowledge is of most worth. As has been highlighted throughout this book, all texts reflect particular ideological assumptions—assumptions that are formed within a society that is structured unequally along lines of human difference. Realizing the democratic ideal, then, requires that the voices of those in the margins be brought to the center. It also requires that we examine the hidden assumptions that are implicit in the texts that we use in our classrooms and in the received knowledge of our respective disciplines. Thus, literacy instruction that is consciously political would involve, first, inviting deliberation on critical social, economic, and political issues, and second, exposing students to the latent values that are embedded in written and oral texts.

A form of instruction that meets these requirements is problem-posing pedagogy, whereby students are presented with questions or problems that have no clear or definitive solutions. Originally conceived by Paulo Freire in his work with Brazilian peasants, problem-posing education challenges students to explore the forces of oppression in their own lives and in society. The intent of this type of pedagogy is to assist students in understanding their situated realities, to engage in critical praxis, so that they might act to transform those realities. Problem-posing education is a dialectical process in which multiple perspectives are actively sought, and students' experiences become a primary source of knowledge for discussion and interrogation.

In his book entitled *Empowering Education* (1992), Ira Shor provides numerous examples of how problem-posing pedagogy can be implemented in classrooms. For instance, in a high school or college literature class, Shor suggests that teachers might begin with a question such as "Is street violence a problem in your lives?" Students would be directed to write about and discuss their answers to this question and interview others about the issue. In class, students would expand their thoughts and the results of their research into written compositions, and these compositions would be used to help students learn about the writing process and the qualities of effective writing, as well as to address the problem of violence in our society. Next, students might be directed to write fictional accounts that describe how individuals try to stop violence in their neighborhood. After discussing, revising, editing, and sharing their stories with their families, final drafts would be published into books and distributed throughout the school and neighborhood.

In addition, Shor suggests that students study the theme of violence in various published texts, for example, "the slave revolt of Spartacus or accounts of Wat Tyler and the peasant revolts of the Middle Ages or *Romeo and Juliet* or *Henry IV* or the Puritan Army debates of the 1640s or chronicles of Columbus pillaging the Native American societies that he found or narratives of slave life and rebellion in the Old South" (p. 82). Shor also suggests that novels such as Hemingway's *For Whom the Bell Tolls,* Malraux's *Man's Fate,* Dickens's *Hard Times,* Piri Thomas's *Down These Mean Streets,* Alice Walker's *The Color Purple,* and Marge Piercy's *Vida* might be used to explore the subject of violence in different historical contexts and settings. Shor would involve persons beyond the classroom by asking students to elicit their families' responses to these texts. Finally, students would be asked to write about changes that would need to occur to confront the problem of violence and how violence might be reduced in their communities. These essays would be sent to the mayor, the chief of police, and local newspapers, and community groups would be invited to come into the classroom to co-develop a plan of action. These activities would help students understand the roots of violence and hatred in our society and the ways in which their own lives might become vehicles for change.

Such instruction is referred to as *situated pedagogy* in that the topics, themes, and issues being examined are situated in students' lives. Thus, students do not experience the alienation typical of traditional pedagogy in which they are asked to memorize facts and receive transmitted information. Situated pedagogy can be contrasted with Freire's notion of "banking" education in which information and reified knowledge is "deposited" in the minds of students (Freire 1970/1993).

To provide further examples of problem-posing pedagogy from Shor's book, a history teacher might begin a course by asking students to explore responses to the question "What is history?" A discussion of this question might be followed by additional questions, such as "What history is most important to you? What do you want to know? Is history getting better or worse than it was in the past?" Shor suggests having students read first-person accounts from a particular time period and examine how past experiences relate to their own lives. Borrowing an idea from Giroux, students might also assume the role of historian by exploring various interpretations of the primary texts and writing their own history from those documents. Through this activity, students come to realize how particular values and perspectives are embedded in written texts. Further, exploring historical themes prior to encountering them in their textbooks—through writing, discussion, and reflection—helps students to personalize a particular time period in history and also "makes it less likely they will be silenced by the teacher's authority or by textbooks in the study of an academic theme" (p. 77). I would suggest that teachers might also include historical fiction and biography to enhance the study of a particular era or theme and provide alternate historical accounts found in books such as Howard Zinn's *A People's History of the United States 1492–Present* (1995), and Ronald Takaki's *A Different Mirror* (1993).

Teachers of other disciplines might begin with similar questions, such as "What is biology?" or "What is math?" and "Why should we study it?" An examination of these questions could lead to a study of issues relevant to students' own lives and to an analysis of conditions within their communities. For instance, a problem-posing science class might study the use of coal and other fossil fuels both in terms of environmental pollution and in terms of their human impact (mine safety, effect on families, etc.). A problem-posing math class might examine the effect of the rising costs of prescription drugs on persons with fixed incomes and explore who benefits from high drug costs. A problem-posing music class might investigate why certain forms of music have been accorded higher status, while other forms are seen as having less aesthetic value. In all of these examples, oral and written language is used to reflect, to challenge, and to examine critically our common-sense notions about the society in which we live.

A useful way of organizing a problem-posing curriculum is to link related concepts around a central theme, such as communication or consumerism. James Banks (1991), for instance, uses the theme of "revolution" to explore resistance through space and time. By organizing content around key interdisciplinary themes, states Banks, "the teacher can structure lessons and units that facilitate the inclusion of content from diverse cultures as well as content that will help students to develop the knowledge, values, commitments, and skills needed to participate in effective personal, economic, and civic action" (p. 133). Banks also presents a value inquiry model that can be used to help students examine their own values about particular issues. This model consists of a series of separate steps and asks students to recognize value problems, determine values that are exemplified by particular behaviors, determine conflicting values, and hypothesize about the possible consequences of making certain value choices. Banks suggests that once students have acquired knowledge about an interdisciplinary concept or issue, they should be asked to engage in a process of values clarification, whereby they can develop a set of consistent values used "to guide purposeful and reflective personal or civic action related to the issue examined" (p. 134).

Building on the principle of thematic teaching, Shor (1992) suggests using topical themes that emerge from the generative themes that are situated in students' lives. One example that is given is a college freshman writing class in which students chose the generative theme "personal growth" as a topic for exploration. Various questions were posed and students reflected on their responses in written essays. Their papers were used as springboards for discussion and to teach specific writing skills. Shor then expanded the students' generative theme with the topical theme, "personal growth is affected by economic policy." Through reading and discussion, students studied the ways in which corporate and government economic policy impacted their personal growth. He also introduced topics of racism and sexism as obstacles to personal growth, and students were invited to write about instances of racism and sexism in their own lives. These writing experiences were followed by a revision of their original essays on personal growth.

Critical literacy, however, need not be limited to the high school or university classroom. In Bob Peterson's fifth grade class, the continuing struggle for social justice is a central theme in the curriculum (Peterson 1994). Peterson uses music, poetry, film, drama, news articles, photos, and other print and media sources to initiate writing and dialogue on particular topics. For instance, he asks his students to dramatize historical events, such as Sojourner Truth's commitment to integrate streetcars after the Civil War, and then asks them to examine contemporary situations where people still face discrimination. He uses the song "New Underground Railroad" with his young students to compare the Underground Railroad of the mid-1800s to the movement to save Jews during World War II and to the sanctuary movement to help refugees from El Salvador in the 1980s, and these discussions are used to stimulate dialogue on anti-Semitism and the U.S. policy in El Salvador. Consistent with the situated learning of problem-posing education, Peterson encourages his students to generate their own questions, which provide the basis for classroom discussion and research. For instance, a common assignment is to have students pose questions from the literature they are reading. Peterson reports that

> while reading *Sidewalk Story* by Sharon Bell Mathis, a children's novel in which the main protagonist, a young girl, struggles to keep her best friend from being evicted, my students posed questions about the ethics of eviction, failure to pay rent, homelessness, discrimination, and the value of material possessions over friendship. (p. 33)

Students arrive at answers and conclusions to their questions through reading about pertinent topics in the literature and through large and small group discussion.

To learn about the nonneutrality of written materials, Peterson's fifth grade students examine written texts for "the messages that are trying to take over your brain" (p. 36) and decide which texts promote justice and fairness. They view films such as *Unlearning Native American Stereotypes* (Council on Interracial Books for Children) and investigate books and classroom materials for bias against Native Americans. Students also compare books for conflicting information and talk about how books can be evaluated for accuracy. Through these and other activities, the students in Bob Peterson's classroom are learning to be "actors in the world, not just things to be acted upon" (p. 38). They are also learning to be moral agents in a society that continues to be characterized by hopelessness and despair.

Another example of problem-posing pedagogy in elementary classrooms is provided by Valerie Ooka Pang (1991). Using a media form that is popular for young students, Pang suggests that children explore the stereotypical messages that are encoded in cartoons. She proposes having students identify the purpose of particular cartoons, look at the ways that the characters are represented and their relationships in the script, and examine the use of language, vocabulary, and voicing techniques. Through these exercises, children can become sensitive to the ways in which cartoons and other media forms send negative hidden messages about particular groups, such as, women are the weaker gender, senior citizens are forgetful, Native Americans are inarticulate. In addition to a study of cartoons, Pang provides other suggestions for elementary students, such as listing stereotypic phrases and discussing their effects, or investigating the concept of justice and applying it to health care issues in their own communities.

In my own work with classroom teachers, students complete activities that are designed to make them aware of the implicit messages found in written texts. For one activity, students are divided into groups, presented with several recently adopted high school textbooks, and directed to examine the ways in which multiple perspectives are presented. With a few rare exceptions, students discover that current textbooks are still overwhelmingly Eurocentric and male; contributions of women and persons of color are either excluded entirely or are reduced to being "mentioned" in a few brief sentences (Apple 1993b). On another occasion, several popular magazines are distributed, and students are instructed to form collaborative groups and to examine the magazines for their implicit cultural assumptions. Merely by taking what seems hidden through its habitualness and making it overt, students quickly realize the ways in which such print media can shape and reinforce taken-for-granted assumptions about human difference. For instance, a popular magazine for young people contains only one picture of an African American teen, and she has characteristically Anglo facial features. A magazine geared for homemakers has pictures of immaculate, professionally designed homes and perfect meals; women students respond that these depictions reinforce middle-class values that suggest that they must be outstanding cooks, interior designers, and housekeepers in order to be valued as wives and mothers. Many of the magazines we examine contain photos of sleek black luxury cars that are owned and driven by (generally White) men clad in dark business suits and toting leather briefcases—images that reinforce popular notions about material success and its relation to class, race, and gender difference. Such images, while they may appear to be neutral and perhaps even innocent, actually serve as a powerful psychological force not only by promoting materialistic (versus democratic or spiritual) rewards, but also by subtly shaping our values and beliefs about who is entitled to those rewards.[4]

A twelfth grade teacher, Audrey Sturk, uses popular print forms in yet another way (Sturk 1992). Choosing controversial articles from newspapers and magazines, her students explore current social and political issues such as illiteracy, vandalism, and wage freezes. Sturk writes that "Our job is to probe deeply into the assumptions behind what is written and to ask who is served by them and how issues can be distorted in the pursuit of personal or class interests" (p. 265). Through these experiences, her students learn how to read critically and how to "take a questioning stance" when they encounter a written text.

In order to motivate students to read, many teachers will endorse the use of magazines and other popular print material in their literature classrooms. It has been my experience, however, that teachers do not recognize or acknowledge the implicit ways in which these print forms tend to marginalize many of their students and to shape their worldviews. Asking students to read such texts critically and to reflect upon the assumptions and values that are embedded in them would challenge students to examine their own beliefs and perspectives. More specifically, what I am suggesting here is that the ideological conflicts that are inherent in the texts we use in our classrooms ought to be made explicit, so that students can enter into the debate and explore the tacit meanings that are being expressed.

It is important to acknowledge that not all students will be receptive to a pedagogy that is consciously political. Some students may prefer to remain passive, while others may actively resist. Often student resistance is the result of the conditioning they have received through prior schooling; they simply are not accustomed to being actively engaged in critical inquiry. Some will find such pedagogy threatening in that it challenges strongly held values and beliefs. Still others may simply not want to disrupt the status quo. For Anglo students, who have benefited and continue to benefit from a system of White privilege, examining implicit ideological assumptions can take them outside of their comfort zones. Bell hooks (1994) writes:

> I teach many white students and they hold diverse political stances. Yet they come into a class on African American women's literature expecting to hear no discussion of the politics of race, class, and gender. Often these students will complain, "Well I thought this was a literature class." What they're really saying to me is, "I thought this class was going to be taught like any other literature class I would take, only we would now substitute black female writers for white male writers." They accept the shift in the locus of representation but resist shifting ways they think about ideas. That is threatening. . . . It's as though many people know that the focus on difference has the potential to revolutionize the classroom and they do not want the revolution to take place. (pp. 144–45)

Teachers who attempt to radicalize their students have often been criticized by both liberals and conservatives alike. Peterson (1994) refers to such criticisms as a fear of the "pied-piper syndrome," the idea that "if teachers promote social activism, they are indoctrinating their students" (p. 40). Certainly, no teacher has the right to impose his or her values on students. However, it is important to differentiate between imposing ideas and providing a forum for critical debate. Shor addresses this concern when he states that

> Students cannot be thought of as a captive audience. If they don't want to discuss a topical theme, they must not be forced to do so. Forced discussion is wholly contradictory to critical-democratic education; it is just another version of the authoritarianism of the traditional school system. No ideals justify indoctrinating students. Their right of refusal must be equal to the teacher's right of presentation. (1992, p. 66)

Thus, while the teacher has the authority to present particular issues for deliberation, she does not have the authority to require student involvement in discussion. The danger of imposing specific beliefs and ideals is also mitigated through the very nature of problem-posing education, which requires a consideration of diverse perspectives through readings, interviews, and class discussions. Indeed, a commitment to democracy is simultaneously a commitment to open dialogue and reciprocal inquiry. Teachers must respect their students' right to embrace particular views, even when those views differ significantly from their own. In this sense, problem-posing education resists indoctrination by providing a forum for the presentation of differing perspectives and by subjecting all ideas to public scrutiny.

It is also imperative, however, that critical teachers view themselves as situated subjects whose own beliefs and cultural assumptions are constrained by their limited experiences. As agents working for change, we must interrogate our own agendas and the motivations behind them. We must acknowledge that as men, women, and members of particular social classes, religious persuasions, and so on, we have multiple subjectivities—subjectivities that are often contradictory and that occasion us to be both the oppressed and the oppressor, often simultaneously. As critical educators, a commitment to illumination requires that we make our own subjectivities objects of critique, that we critically examine our deeply held ideological assumptions, and that we be willing to accept that, in the final analysis, we might be wrong.

## CONCLUSION

Presenting a counterdiscourse requires that our teaching be consciously political. Teaching practices that are consciously political make visible what was previously hidden and render problematic what was previously taken for granted.

Through a counterhegemonic, critical pedagogy, both students and teachers come to understand how language and cultural knowledge are used to privilege and oppress. Teachers and students are challenged to interrogate their cultural assumptions and to examine their ideological perspectives by becoming coparticipants in investigating the dynamics of cultural production and power.

Some would argue that we have no right to present a consciously political agenda in our classrooms. I, too, have struggled with this issue. As teachers, we certainly have the right—indeed, we have an obligation—to present diverse points of view. Yet, do we have the right to raise issues associated with equity, social justice, and oppression? Do we have the right to challenge our students to confront the hegemonic order, to render problematic a system of meritocracy from which many of them have benefited? Do we have the right to ask them to delve into the sources of personal and institutionalized racism, sexism, homophobia? Do we have the right to encourage them to explore issues associated with hopelessness and despair, to analyze the ways in which they may assume contradictory roles as both victimizer and victim, to confront their own silence? The decision to take a consciously political stance is not an easy one; certainly, it is easier to hide under a facade of neutrality.

Yet, if our goal is for a more just and equitable society—one that is grounded in compassion and care, one that is less violent and more hopeful for our children and for our children's children, one that cherishes our collective humanity and common destiny—then the answer to these questions must be yes. These are moral questions that require a moral response. Our society demands nothing less.

Society requires much of its schools, and schools require much from educators. Our efforts will necessarily be only partial. It is important for those of us who strive to implement a more emancipatory literacy to acknowledge that not all of the information students must acquire in schools lends itself to a critical pedagogy; often, our teaching may look very noncritical. Nevertheless, I would argue that there are spaces in all of our classrooms where transformation can potentially be realized—spaces where students can take risks, test hypotheses, and challenge their taken-for-granted assumptions about the world.

In this chapter, I suggest ways for making classrooms places where the dominant ideology can be resisted and where alternative rationalities can become realized. I also argue that we ought not conceal this political agenda; indeed, to do so would deny the goal of illumination that critical literacy seeks to realize. Teachers who embrace a critical literacy are taking sides toward a less oppressive and more equitable society. If we are to avoid subversive pedagogy ourselves—the very type of pedagogy that we seek to eliminate—then we must reveal this agenda to our students, and we must acknowledge their right to take an alternate stance.

Further, critical teachers must recognize that all knowledge, including their own, will always be partial. We cannot, in the words of Knoblauch and Brannon (1993), claim a "transcendent power of insight" and forget our own "ideological situatedness" (p. 165). At the same time that we ask students to deconstruct the texts of schooled literacy and of society, we must also deconstruct our own. The liberatory agendas of critical educators can be problematic; more is said about this issue in the next chapter.

Finally, it is important to acknowledge that not all students will be receptive to the critical, "proper" form of literacy that I espouse in this chapter, nor will all students feel "empowered" through critical literacy (Ellsworth 1989). In fact, as Hourigan (1994) points out, resistance may come not merely from upper-class students, who may prefer to remain oblivious to their own privileged status, but also from working-class or nonmainstream students who do not want to acknowledge the inequities that exist between themselves and those in power. Thus, there are tensions in classrooms that seek to be both democratic and liberatory, for a democratic classroom requires that students be given the option of rejecting our efforts to introduce controversial subjects.

Teachers, too, for a variety of reasons, often tend to resist a pedagogy that is consciously political and that provides for more egalitarian relationships with their students. Conditioned by years of banking education, some educators are reluctant to relinquish control. Even teachers who desire to provide their students with a more proper, critical literacy often find that they are constrained by the technical and bureaucratic control that is inherent in the culture of schooling and fear reprisals by administrators, other teachers, and members of the community (Eller 1989a).[5] These constraints are very real for all of us, and therefore we must acknowledge that our efforts in schools will remain only partial, and that our hope for transformation must inevitably carry us beyond the walls of our classrooms.

Nevertheless, it is important to emphasize that remaining silent with the intent of appearing neutral is at best a questionable practice. Our pedagogical options are already political; to quote Peterson, "Even a teacher who consciously attempts to be politically 'neutral' makes hundreds of political decisions—from the posters on the wall to attitudes toward holidays" (p. 40). Not only is taking a neutral stance largely a facade, but it also creates apathy and indifference, which merely perpetuates the status quo. As Gerald Graff (1992) argues, a "frank discussion of . . . conflicts is more likely to improve our handling of them than pretending they do not exist" (p. 33). By becoming consciously political, we no longer hide behind a cloak of innocence.

Preparing students for democratic participation requires that we resist indifference and engage them in political debate. Life itself is not value-free but rather is driven by controversy that has its roots in class, race, and gender struggle. Hence, it is important that all students—men, women, Anglos, persons of color—come to understand the ways in which they have been damaged by a system of unearned privilege (McIntosh 1988). Castenell and Pinar (1993) argue that the traditional curriculum ought to be viewed as a "racial text," one that distorts our history as a pluralistic society and denies our cultural reality as a nation. Such distortion not only affects marginalized populations, but it also has a negative effect on White students, for it allows them to remain oblivious to their own privileged status. "By refusing to understand curriculum as racial text," suggest the authors, "students misunderstand that they are also racialized, gendered, historical, political creatures. Such deformity occurs—for most 'whites'—almost 'unconsciously'" (p. 6). Thus, for nonmainstream students, ignoring or denying the hegemonic function of written and oral texts often reinforces an illusion of their own inferiority, while for many mainstream students, it reinforces the delusion of their own superiority. What is needed is a curriculum that problematizes difference, that uncovers our hidden suppositions about the relationship between human difference and a system of meritocracy. This is precisely what literacy instruction that is consciously political is designed to do.

## NOTES

1. I do not believe that Gee is suggesting that one cannot master secondary discourses; rather, he is suggesting that discourses cannot be mastered solely through direct instruction in the form and superficial features of language—those aspects of language that are typically "learned" in classrooms. Gee also is careful to point out that teaching form is important and necessary (see Gee 1990, p. 162), but it should not overshadow an understanding of the hegemonic function of language.

2. In fact, Gee defines literacy as the "mastery of, or fluent control over, a secondary Discourse" (1990, p. 153).

3. Just as problematic is the tendency of some educators to view students' primary discourse as inferior and to associate that inferiority with overall incompetence. Such perceptions often lead to self-fulfilling prophecies. Furthermore, denigrating a student's language further alienates nonstandard speakers, who already are victims of marginalization in schools. Thus I would suggest that teachers, too, must learn about the social and cultural dimensions of language use, so that they can recognize their students' linguistic competence and can provide appropriate learning experiences for their students. For a more complete discussion of teachers' perceptions of students' language use, see my discussion in *The Reading Teacher* (Eller 1989b; reprinted in Opitz 1998).

4. An excellent resource for high school English teachers is *Cultural Reflections: Critical Teaching and Learning in the English Classroom* (1997), written by high school teacher John Gaughan. In this book, Gaughan describes how he helps his students to "read the world" through a critical examination of the cultural assumptions implicit in language use, films, commercials, and so on.

5. Shor and Freire (1987) discuss the need for teachers to acquire "deviance credits" so that they can be "recognized as a legitimate part of the scenery" within the school (p. 66). By taking on a variety of institutional tasks, teachers are able to accumulate "credits" that allow them more room to "deviate."

# 6

# Toward a Transformative Vision

Without a vibrant tradition of resistance passed on to new generations, there can be no nurturing of a collective and critical consciousness—only professional conscientiousness survives. Where there is no vital community to hold up precious ethical and religious ideals, there can be no coming to a moral commitment—only personal accomplishment is applauded. Without a credible sense of political struggle, there can be no shouldering of a courageous engagement—only cautious adjustment is undertaken. (Cornel West, *Race Matters,* pp. 56–57)

The root meaning of "objective" is "to put against, to oppose." This is the danger of objectivism: it is a way of knowing that places us in an adversary relation to the world. By this view, we are not required to change so that the whole community might flourish; instead, the world must change to meet our needs. Indeed, objectivism has put us in an adversary relation to one another. The oppression of cultural minorities by a white, middle-class, male version of "truth" comes in part from the domineering mentality of objectivism. Once the objectivist has "the facts," no listening is required, no other points of view are needed. The facts, after all, are the facts. All that remains is to bring others into conformity with objective "truth."

The view that truth is personal leads neither to objective imperialism nor subjective relativism. Instead, truth is found as we are obedient to a pluralistic reality, as we engage in that patient process of dialogue, consensus seeking, and personal transformation in which all parties subject themselves to the bonds of communal troth. Such a way of knowing is more likely to bridge our gaps and divisions than drive us farther apart. Such a way of knowing can help heal us and our broken world. (Parker Palmer, *To Know As We Are Known,* p. 68)

Our conceptualization of empowerment is generally grounded in an objective rationalism that privileges individual knowers and seekers of truth. Knowledge is power; it enables us to control our personal destinies, to own our respective futures, to reconstruct our autonomous realities. The power of analytic knowing allows us to dissect our world and to uncover objective truths. It permits us to act rationally in our interactions with others, to engage in systematic inquiry, and to *act on* the world as we seek to transform it.

Yet, there is something inherently troubling about reigning notions of empowerment, for an empowerment that emerges from objective rationalism has the potential of re-creating the very inequities we seek to eliminate. Framed within an epistemology of chronic individualism, its tendency is merely to rearrange but not to transform, to result in cautious adjustment rather than substantive change. The prevailing language of empowerment endorses individual advancement and personal fulfillment at the expense of collective action. It is a language that opens the door of opportunity while obstructing the entrance for others, that illuminates reality while denying our subjective voice, that applauds personal accomplishment while ignoring a social mission.

To be truly transformative, empowerment must be linked to a moral vision that insists on justice and equity for all. It is a vision that is grounded in a culture of compassion and care, that emerges from a collective identity united through common aims. Roger Simon (1992) states that a pedagogy of empowerment

> must ask the question: empowerment for what? This, I want to emphasize, is the site of the insufficiency of the term empowerment. Without a vision for the future a pedagogy of empowerment is reduced to a method for participation which takes democracy as an end and not a means! There is no moral vision other than the insistence on people having an equal claim to a place in the public arena. (pp. 143–44)

An emancipatory literacy releases us from the bondage of disillusionment, inciting us to challenge the immobilizing forces of inertia that surround us and pursue new avenues for resistance. It is a literacy that legitimizes all voices, that affirms students' languages, and that penetrates the invisibility of hegemony. Yet, as an emancipatory tool, this literacy will remain inadequate if its goal is limited to personal liberation and not social transformation. A transformative literacy embraces a "project of possibility"—"a particular moral project, a particular 'not yet' of how we might live our lives together" (Simon 1992, p. 141).

## REALIZING A TRANSFORMATIVE LITERACY

To use the eloquent words of Cornel West, a transformative literacy nurtures "a collective and critical consciousness"; it encourages a "vital community" that is committed to moral aims and religious and ethical ideals; and it calls for "courageous engagement" in the political struggle for equity and justice. To become truly transformative, a literacy for empowerment must provide more than equal opportunity for individual advancement; it must be linked to a larger social commitment that is grounded in a culture of compassion and care. Parker Palmer (1993) uses the term *troth* to capture the type of relationship that is required for transformation:

> With this word one person enters a covenant with another, a pledge to engage in a mutually accountable and transforming relationship, a relationship forged of trust and faith in the face of unknowable risks. . . . We find truth by pledging our troth, and knowing becomes a reunion of separated beings whose primary bond is not of logic but of love. (pp. 31–32)

In our pedantic academic circles, we are unaccustomed to talking about transformation in such terms. In our quest for professional objectivism, we tend to avoid words like *love* that would cast us into the metaphysical realm, that would make us appear unscholarly or even melodramatic. Yet in so doing, we deny the part of our existence that excites our imagination, that inspires us to reach new levels of creativity, that dares us to be whole. We also deny the forces of passion and pain that join us as a human race and that compel us to work for justice—that enable us to forge transforming relationships that make systemic change possible.

Students must see that their words can become a voice of resistance that can help to overcome social barriers to change. In the pages that follow, I argue that students must become aware of the power of language—*their language*—for transformation. At the same time, however, a literacy that empowers is not enough. To be truly transformative, the power of their words must be motivated by love, by agape, by the desire to make all persons free.

### Criterion No. 4: Literacy Ought to Be Taught in Ways that Make Students Aware of the Power of Language for Transformation

What differentiates progressive literacy instruction from critical or transformative literacy instruction are their goals. Progressive literacy instruction is concerned with the "best" methodology for teaching students to "read the word"; critical pedagogy, in contrast, is committed to helping students "read the world" at the same time that they learn to "read the word" (Shor and Freire 1987; Freire and Macedo 1987; Macedo 1994). Progressive literacy instruction has as its primary aim learning to read, write, and comprehend written texts. Critical literacy instruction has as its primary aim the ability to use oral and written texts for liberatory purposes. While progressive literacy instruction is informed by linguistic theory, critical pedagogy is informed by political debate.

Throughout the ages, members of our society who have been marginalized through oppressive social, economic, and political structures have used the power of words to transform and inspire. In her book *Other People's Children* (1995), Lisa Delpit acknowledges the need to teach language in a way that makes its hegemonic function visible, so that it can be used for liberation. It is worth quoting her at length here:

> [Teachers] must understand that students who appear to be unable to learn are in many instances choosing to "not-learn" as Kohl puts it, choosing to maintain their sense of identity in the face of what they perceive as a painful choice between allegiance to "them" or "us." The teacher, however, can reduce this sense of choice by transforming the new discourse so that it contains within it a place for the students' selves. To do so, they must saturate the dominant discourse with new meaning, must wrest from it a place for the glorification of their students and their forbears. . . . [Such teachers] also seek to teach students about those who have taken the language born in Europe and transformed it into an emancipatory tool for those facing oppression in the "new world." In the mouths and pens of Bill Trent, Clarence Cunningham, bell hooks, Henry Louis Gates, Paul Lawrence Dunbar and countless others, the "language of the master" has been used for liberatory ends. (pp. 163–65)

It is this use of language as an emancipatory tool that I am arguing we must share with our students through the ways in which we teach and use language in our classrooms.

For a transformative literacy to be realized, students must believe that their words will be heard, and that the hearing of their words can have the potential not just to inform, but also to inspire. They must believe that their ideas can contribute to the formation and realization of a moral vision, and that their voices can stir the imagination, awaken the passion within us, and penetrate our souls. In essence, a transformative literacy is one that leads students to feel the authority of language for their own lives, and to trust in the power of their words to affect change.

For literacy to be transformative, oral and written language must have personal relevancy for students. They must be able to see themselves in written and oral texts; they must believe that language has meaning for them. To use the metaphor coined by Frank Smith (1988), they must view themselves as members of the "literacy club"—as real readers and writers whose experiences are reflected in the words they read and whose own words can speak to others. Oliver (1994) writes that "one of the most destructive features of maintaining the literary canon as a white, male-dominated corpus is the denial of the existence of other literary works. Thus, students of color and others who do not fit into the mainstream are always on the outside looking in" (p. 10). For literacy to be personally meaningful, it must validate students' identities by speaking to their experiences, dreams, and desires (Au 1993; Oliver 1994; Willis 1998).

Books that are culturally authentic, that portray realistic and nonstereotypical representations of nonmainstream groups, can help students to realize that literacy can be an important part of their lives.[1] Such books provide opportunities for students to read about their own realities as they are mirrored in the texts. Teachers who are committed to using multicultural and multiethnic literature report that students often respond positively to these books and tend to read them with an increased level of engagement (Oliver 1994; Spears-Bunton 1990, 1996). For instance, in her study of the introduction of African American literature in one high school English classroom, Spears-Bunton shares the story of Troy, an African American student who was the leader of a racially mixed group called the "Fellas." Early in the study, Troy "joked and failed harmoniously" with the other members of the group; however, he began to take an interest in the African American literature being read in the class and subsequently began receiving honors-level grades. He also "removed himself physically from the Fellas' corner when he wanted to read or work on an assignment." Spears-Bunton reports that

> in interviews, Troy expressed the view that this literature was part of his culture and was distinct from other literature in "language, rituals, themes and in the presentation of life" offered by the text. He added, "everybody has a culture; I just don't know my culture. I guess I've been too lazy to find out." For students like Troy, the use of African-American literature led to a reassessment of school, peer relationships, and self. (1996, p. 65)

Other students in the class—including European American students—were also affected by the study of African American literature. While the focus of the African American students was upon self-discovery and issues of identity, the European American students "moved toward the discovery of and respect for the unique humanity of others." Spears-Bunton states that pejorative jokes and comments that had previously helped solidify the Fellas were no longer viewed as acceptable. Later, when a White member of the Fellas suggested that "me and my friends think just alike, about everything," Troy shook his head and replied "no man, it ain't like that, and it just ain't right disrespecting people like that." For Troy, as for other students in the class, learning about themselves through African American literature gave them the power to resist domination and to work for change.

Literature can help students as they struggle with identity issues and attempt to find their places in the world. By capturing diverse realities, multicultural/multiethnic literature enables students to see their own lives through an acceptable lens, thereby validating their cultural experiences. Beyond this, however, texts that reflect our human diversity can help students to know themselves through examining their relations with others. African American author Mildred Pitts Walter admonishes us to "seek out people who are different, so you can truly know who you are" (quoted in Day 1994,

p. 184). We come to understand ourselves by exploring our differences and by learning about the experiences of others. Hence, multicultural literature can be particularly valuable for European American students, many of whom have never endured the pain of rejection and alienation that comes from being the Other.

More important to a critical theory of literacy, however, is the value of multicultural literature to reveal the transformative power of language. Students must be able to read the words and hear the voices of those who are like themselves and who have used language to fight against oppression: Ralph Ellison, Rudolfo Anaya, Toni Morrison, Jimmy Santiago Baca, Langston Hughes, Maya Angelou, Richard Wright, Martin Luther King Jr., Elie Wiesel, and hundreds of others who have written with passion and candor about the human experience. Students must be led to realize that they are heirs to a rich literary tradition that is not bound by human difference, that they are part of a heritage of writers who have used the spoken and written word to make their voices heard around the world. Reading books written by culturally and ethnically diverse authors will teach nonmainstream students that the literacy club is not exclusionary, and that they, too, can use literacy as an instrument for liberatory ends.

Students can also learn about the power of language for transformation through writing. For writing to be liberating, students must be positioned as "subjects" (Edelsky 1991); that is, they must be allowed to write from their own experiences, using written language to capture the important moments of their lives. High school teacher and author Randy Bomer (1995) states that a student is literate when he uses language "in the construction of meaning from his own lived life" (p. 9). Writing is used to help students to interrogate their lives, to "craft sense." A number of writing educators encourage students to keep notebooks—or what Lucy Calkins aptly calls "lifebooks"—to record daily observations and events so that writing will become an organic extension of their lives (Bomer 1995; Calkins 1994; Calkins and Harwayne 1991). Even very young children can "gather the treasures of their lives" in notebooks, to develop a habit of "wide-awakedness" and a sense of wonderment about the world. Calkins (1994) writes that

> we grown-ups do not have to teach young children to cherish the little stuff of their lives. We do not have to remind them to cup their hands around the bits of their lives and declare them treasures. . . . What we do need is to teach children that their wonderings and questions and curiosity are part of what it means to write well. (p. 94)

Looking at our students' worlds and allowing those worlds to penetrate the classroom can result in powerful writing. Consider the voice of eight-year-old Melissa, who writes about her memories of the death of her grandmother:

One day my nanny got real sick. Every day me and my Mom had to go up and take care of her. The next day she was worse than the day before. A while after that she tried to go to the bathroom and when she was finished she slipped and fell. She fainted. We could not wake her up. Finally she came to. My Dad called the hospital and got an ambulance. My cousin Stevie took me down to his house. About two hours later my Mom and Dad came and told me that she had died of a heart attack. I cried for a long time. Me and My Nanny used to go shopping. She taught me to play cards and she taught me to cook. She was the best person in the world. Happy Easter Nanny! (*Great Mountain Tales,* 1989, p. 27)

Consider, too, the words of seventeen-year-old Tony, as he shares the troubling experience of his mixed heritage in a world that continues to be racially constituted:

> For my people of the mixed race.
> We are not mutts, or imperfections,
> in an already imperfect world.
> Poisonous by-products of two races,
> we are not here to pollute society,
> a society already polluted,
> with the waste of hatred.
> High yellow is not our label.
> We are all shades.
> From a cocoa brown to a golden honey,
> a rich red, to a faint yellow,
> we are a rainbow of browns.
>
> We are forced to choose a box,
> deny our mother or father.
> Categorized into a society,
> where only black, white,
> Mexican, and Asian are acknowledged.
>
> So what are we?
> Where is the box,
> the box that gives us identity?
> We don't need a box to tell us
> who we are.
>
> We are the best,
> of two, four, or more worlds.
> We are the true melting pots.
> And one day we'll have a box.
>
> (Tony Melson,
> "A Box of Our Own"
> in *Rites of Passage,* 1994–95)

Finally, consider the words of high school senior Qiana Davis, who through reading the words of other African American writers has learned about the power of her own voice:

> When people stare and look at me,
> They search and glare,
> But still can't see:
> It's the bulk of my mind,
> The braids in my hair.
> I am a black woman,
> And I'm talking about all
> Of me.
>
> It's the Ebony of my skin,
> The swell of my hips,
> The Ivory of my teeth,
> And the ripeness of my lips.
> I am a black woman,
> And I'm talking about all
> Of me.
>
> It's hidden in my soul,
> So they still can't see.
> It's in the innocence of my eyes.
> The experience of my mind.
> The depth of my thoughts.
> The power of my pen.
>
> It's in the strength of my voice.
> The pride in myself.
> The weight of my heart.
> And the power of my words.
>
> Black woman.
> Deep woman.
> Every woman.
> That's me.
>
> (Qiana Davis,
> "Ebony Woman,"
> in *Rites of Passage*, 1994–95)

When we draw upon students' experiences and imaginations in the writing classroom, we validate their lives. We make significant those everyday events that otherwise might appear trivial or mundane; we allow students to make meaning and claim it as their own. We teach them that their lives matter, and that what they write can make a difference. In other words, we teach them the power of language.

We also teach students the power of language when we give them real reasons to write, and real audiences to hear their words. The second grade students in Karen Owsley's classroom in eastern Kentucky learned about the power of language when they developed their own radio show and talked about events and issues that mattered to them. The Appalachian students in Bill McLean's middle school social studies class learned about the power of language when they wrote and spoke publicly on important issues in their lives—environmental pollution, the "hillbilly image," acid rain—and when they were subsequently interviewed by reporters from a national television network (Eller 1989a)[2]. The students in Audrey Sturk's high school English class in Nova Scotia learned about the power of language when their research essays on senior citizens resulted in various collaborative efforts to improve the lives of the elderly in their community, including the closing of a nursing home that was in violation of residents' rights (Sturk 1992). In all of these instances, students' voices extended beyond the classroom, and they learned that their words can matter.

In a moving account of his experiences as a collaborative writing teacher in the New York City public schools, Stephen O'Connor documents his efforts to help his students understand the transformative potential of language (O'-Connor 1996). Through various writing assignments, O'Connor's middle school students explored the tragedy of death and violence that for each of them had become a daily reality. Writing was used in ways that, in O'Connor's words, helped his students "gain a deeper understanding of some of the most dangerous and troubling things in their lives so that they might be better able to rise above them" (p. 380). Their written pieces were combined into plays that were later performed for the community. One play begins with a verse written by Ian Moore, who was later to be killed at the age of seventeen:

> What I fear began when my grandmother
>  died
> Obviously, it was the fear of death
> Death is something I just can't handle
> I fear death because I don't know
> What will happen when I go
> It is something I can't face
> When I die, will I be thought about?
> Will my name be shouted out?
> Death will come at any time
> No matter how far you're up the ladder. (p. 290)

For these students, both oral and written texts had become a means for examining their lives within a society that is socially structured along artificial boundaries of race, class, gender, and other forms of human difference. Yet throughout his book, O'Connor concedes the limitation of education for changing society, acknowledging the pervasiveness of hegemonic forces that operate to maintain an underclass. Nevertheless, he remains committed to the power of literacy for emancipation:

> [The students] talked about the issues raised in the writing: about whether it was right to kill for self-protection, about whether it was practical to turn the other cheek, about how people lie to themselves and can be cruel to the ones they love. . . . They did things they never thought they could do. They created works of art by working together. . . . All of my students, the actors and the writers, gained memories that they will have for the rest of their lives. I did too.
>
> This is literature—not just the reading and the writing, but the thinking, feeling, living, and remembering. This is how literature "matters" most, how it can shape individual lives and even change the world. (pp. 381–82)

It is this gift of literature that we must strive to offer our students—a gift that celebrates students' voices and teaches them that their voices can make a difference.

I end this section with one final story. It is a story about teachers who discovered that their voices can matter in a society that has been torn apart by oppression and violence. Shelley Harwayne recounts the time that she and her daughter met with 150 Black educators from South Africa who were participants in a writing institute in Soweto. Having searched the library shelves in several schools for South African literature and finding none, Harwayne commissioned the educators to write the stories that had not yet been told: "write for yourselves, and for the children of South Africa, and for the teachers and children of the world who need to hear you." Following this pronouncement,

> A stillness greatened in that room as the South African teachers wrote about a father detained in prison for eight years. They wrote of urine trickling down their legs because no nearby shopkeeper would allow them to use the toilet. They wrote poems about a brother disabled in a mining accident and folktales about beasts and jungle boys, wise men and witch doctors. They wrote poems and chants and shows, too, for the market theater, and they wrote an Izibonga song, a South African song of praise performed at funerals and workers' rallies and on other special occasions. They wrote with urgency and rigor because they wrote about topics that matter and they wrote for people and occasions and causes that matter. (Calkins and Harwayne 1991, p. 107)

These teachers wrote with urgency because they understood the significance of language for transformation and had been led to see how their own words could affect change. Merely teaching the nonneutrality of texts is not enough; rather, students and teachers must see the transformative potential of literacy for their own lives and for society. Literacy has emancipatory potential when it evokes a moral response—a response that inspires not individual liberation, but freedom and justice for all.

In this discussion, I suggest that students must become cognizant of the power of their own language for transformation. A point that should be reiterated here is that a literacy that encourages the student voice but fails to demonstrate how that voice can become a source for constructive change is one that is essentially immobilizing. Such a literacy advocates only individual response to the many social ills that plague us—issues that will require collective action to resist and to transform—and thereby contributes to a state of hopelessness and acquiescence. A literacy that sanctions only individual action will obscure the divide and conquer syndrome, the pervasive tendency to view our problems as isolated ones that require only limited, individual solutions, rather than as collective problems that affect us as a society. In the words of classroom teacher Bill Bigelow, we need to do more than "just encourage students to stage a literary show-and-tell"; rather, we must help students to "find meaning in individual experience—to push students to use their stories as windows not only on their lives, but on society" (1992, p. 74). What is required is a literacy that politicizes human difference and that encourages us to join forces against institutionalized oppression—one that reveals that, collectively, we can make a difference.

### Criterion No. 5: Literacy Ought to Be Taught in Ways that Nurture a Culture of Compassion and Care

At the same time that we are teaching students the power of their own words to transform, we must ask the critical question: "transformation for what ends?" One of the exercises I give my graduate students is to visualize an ideal society. They are to list attributes that would characterize a world toward which we might strive, a world that they would like to leave to future generations. Invariably, a central response of these teachers is to call for a society that is characterized by an ethic of caring. Reminiscent of Nel Noddings's ideas about the caring relationship (1992, 1995), the ethic that they envision encompasses not only caring for others who are known, but also caring for distant others and for the whole living kingdom. The next assignment I give them is to provide one or two ideas for how schools might help us to realize a more compassionate, caring, and equitable society. Of the two tasks, this is obviously the more difficult, for it requires us to engage our imaginations, to resist the deceptive current of the mainstream, to look beyond the ordinary. That is, it requires a transformative vision. Hence our responses often tend to be trivial, for they offer neither significant challenges nor substantive alternatives to the status quo.

I would argue that the primary reason for the lack of a truly transformative response to the problems that plague both education and society is that—through either a narrow perspective or limited faith, or both—we have failed to create an alternative vision for what society might become. The news media constantly reminds us that mankind has the capacity for tremendous destruction and malice. Such unremitting images of man's demonic nature lead us down a road of despair—one where hope is annihilated, and where narcissistic pleasure becomes a substitute for deeper communion and commitment. Further, the pervasiveness of a technocratic, Cartesian rationality limits our capacity for seeing the world differently, for entering into relationships of troth, for envisioning a society where the degree of our compassion might become the ultimate yardstick for measuring our worth as a people and a nation. Our obsession with the objective and the physical, with material and technological solutions versus metaphysical ones, suppresses our ability to discover untapped realities. Yet surely the world cries out for answers that go beyond mere technological insights and are grounded in principles of love and care. What I am suggesting here is that perhaps developing an ethic of caring ought to be an educational aim that is considered to be at least as important as assuring the expansion of economic and technological achievements; for human evolution depends primarily upon developing caring relationships, not upon enhancing our ability to control.

Thus far I have argued that a proper literacy is one that empowers students and teachers and that furthers a democratic community through the equitable distribution of power. Empowerment through a proper, critical literacy encourages us to enter the fray, to engage in a liberatory struggle. Yet it is important to state that this struggle is not so much a political one as a *moral* one. Its outcomes are not personal power, but equity; not individual liberation, but social justice. Thus, a proper literacy is also one that nurtures an ethic of caring, for it is through relationships of care—through love, or agape—that we are driven to eliminate oppression and to work for the *common* good. Only agape can mitigate the problems associated with narcissism, whereby the liberation of one can lead to the oppression of another. Only agape can reveal the limitations of our egocentric visions and our own potential to oppress. And it is only through agape that we will be motivated to sacrifice our individual interests and to work for the greater good.

Schooled literacy, which is embedded in a technocratic, objectivist rationality, tends to divide rather than unite, to alienate rather than affirm. What is required is a literacy that provides for emotional and spiritual response and that helps us understand our human connectedness, that validates the worth of every individual, and that mobilizes us to work for change. It is a literacy that has as its primary goal the forging of a vital moral community—a goal that is realized not only through empowerment and illumination, but through the development of relations of care.

Nel Noddings writes that caring is not just a "warm feeling" but is a moral commitment to others, a reciprocal relationship between the one caring and the one cared for (Kendrick 1994; Noddings 1992). That is, caring is a "way of being in relation" rather than a specific set of behaviors (Noddings 1992,

p. 17), a way of knowing that "becomes a reunion of separated beings whose primary bond is not of logic but of love" (Palmer 1993, p. 32). In the pages that follow, I examine a literacy that cultivates an ethic of care. I suggest that such a literacy must be one where all voices are heard, where children's language and experiences are shared and affirmed, and where each child is able to contribute in positive ways to the growth of others within the community. It is also a literacy that unites us toward common goals and that encourages us to work toward a collective vision.

To develop an ethic of care, we must "concentrate on developing the attitudes and skills required to sustain caring relations and the desire to do so" (Noddings 1992, pp. 21–22). Noddings suggests that a moral education that nurtures a culture of care has four primary components: modeling, dialogue, practice, and confirmation. Modeling requires that, as teachers, "we show [our students] how to care by creating caring relations with them" (p. 22). Dialogue "connects us to each other and helps to maintain caring relations. It also provides us with the knowledge of each other that forms a foundation for response in caring" (p. 23). Practice is necessary for developing the capacity to care, for inducing "certain attitudes and ways of looking at the world" (p. 23). Finally, confirmation "lifts us toward our vision of a better self" (p. 25). It is an act of affirmation, a "loving act founded on a relation of some depth" that can only be realized "if we know the other well enough to see what he or she is trying to become" (pp. 25, 24). In the pages that follow, I examine how these components can be used to conceptualize a literacy program that promotes a culture of compassion and care.

## Modeling

It seems almost trite to suggest that we ought to love our students. To love them, however, requires that we know them at a personal level, and that we become vulnerable enough so that we can enter into a mutual relationship of care. As I state in earlier chapters, schooled literacy undermines the formation of caring relationships by establishing boundaries and promoting distance between teachers and students. Students are viewed as empty vessels to be filled, rather than as individuals who come with rich linguistic and cultural experiences. To develop relationships of care with the students we teach, we must personalize our classrooms; we must fill our rooms with their stories, their hopes, their aspirations; we must learn to love them.

Caring about our students requires that we be willing to enter into their lives—to learn about the painful experiences as well as the joyous ones, to help them to overcome their failures and to join with them in celebrating their triumphs. We must constantly observe our students, enter into conversations with them, hear their stories, and document the events of their lives, so that we can develop a comprehensive portrait of their realities. As teachers, our relationship with our students must become one of trust and mutual regard; we can no longer remain aloof and distant but must risk forming a more equitable relationship—one that is grounded in compassion and care.

In order to enter into students' lives, we must really listen to them. Our responses to their experiences cannot be trivial, for superficial responses convey that we have not really heard them, that their experiences are insignificant, that their stories are not worth sharing. Rather, when we truly listen to the narratives of our students, we enter into a relationship with them: we laugh with them, cry with them, celebrate with them, feel their anger and their pain. Lucy Calkins (1994) shares an event that occurred at a staff development workshop that underscores the need for teachers to be "human" when we respond to students' written texts:

> "Here is my story. I'm done," I announced and on an overhead projector I displayed the draft:
> One time my grandfather was in the hospital. He didn't get any better. So he went to God. I miss my grandfather.
> Hands went up as members of the audience took the part of the teacher. "What did the hospital look like?" one woman asked. Still others wanted to know what it had been like when my grandfather was alive. A woman said no, she would ask if the draft was done, did I plan to revise it? After many such responses, someone timidly said, "This probably isn't the right response, but to tell the truth, I'd hug the child and say I was sorry her grandfather died."
> Why is it so difficult to give a simple human response? I think it is because we try so hard to be helpful we forget to be real. (pp. 231–32)

Elsewhere, Calkins states: "As we move around the room hearing our students' stories, our teaching changes our children—and it changes us. Each child becomes infinitely precious to us" (p. 17). When we invite students to share their lives with us and when we risk "being real" as teachers, the richness of their lives will often astound us—and we will learn to love them.

To develop mutual relations of care, teachers must risk being human in the classroom. One of my favorite authors is writing researcher Donald Graves. The joy he feels for life and the love he has for the children he teaches comes through in the pages he has written. In the writing workshop, Graves becomes a co-participant with his students by routinely sharing moments of his own life through his writing. In a mini-lesson on topic selection, for example, Graves tells them, "'I remember once my mother sent me to my room because I hadn't done my chores.' 'What were your chores?' they ask. 'Oh, we had to take turns doing the dishes. I was a boy and I didn't think that was right'" (Graves 1994, p. 55). As a way to introduce students to the idea of portfolios, he shares favorite family photographs that he has gathered over the years. On another day, to model a new record-keeping system, he tells them about several pieces of his own writing: "Take the first one, 'Dog's Shedding.' In this one I really wrote a strong opinion piece. I was just fed up with picking up all the hair around the house"; and a special letter he had written to his father: "He's been sick and I wanted him to know I cared about him and that I understood about his sickness" (pp. 157–58).

We model caring relationships with students when we are willing to share stories from our own lives. By revealing our innermost thoughts and feelings, such stories allow our students to reach out to us, an important factor in an authentic relationship of reciprocal care. Consider the words that teacher Isoke Nia shared with her students about her experiences as a foster child:

> I watched with my small oval Black face tilted as her cocoa-colored hands kneaded the dough. No wonder those biscuits tasted so good. They were loved. At that moment I felt jealous. Envious of the flour, the shortening, the baking powder, the salt, the milk that formed the white lump my foster mother so carefully caressed. I longed to be a white shapeless lump, instead of a tiny Black child. To be void of form and content instead of filled with ideas and feelings and notions and love. I wanted out of my Blackness, my smallness, myself. I wanted a HUG. No hug was given that Sunday or any Sunday to follow. And though all living things need love to grow, I grew regardless. At age 15, I surprised everyone who didn't know me (and that was everyone) by leaving. Biscuits just weren't enough anymore.
>
> The four years that followed contained one day each. And on each of those four days I did something special for me. On day 1, I discovered my Africaness and I clothed myself with the pride of my ancestors and America became tolerable. On day 2, I met a man who was to be the father of my children and on day 3 and 4 I gave birth and was loved and loved and loved . . . and made biscuits on Sunday. (Calkins and Harwayne 1991, pp. 55–56)

In sharing this story of her distressed childhood with the children she teaches, Nia is inviting her students to do the same—inviting them to risk being human, to risk sharing their joys and heartaches, to risk being loved.

Loving our students, however, is often painful. High school teacher Randy Bomer (1995) shares the story of Jerry, who "shouldn't be losing teeth at fourteen,"

> But last week, he walked in with a big gap in the front of his mouth and was evasive about how it got there. I interpreted. From his notebook and from conversations with him, I know that his family has more or less rented him to a farmer. He works, beginning long before I am awake and often late into the night, and his family gets the money. He sleeps in an upstairs room in the house on the farm, a room in which plastic covers the gaping holes where windows should be, especially in an upstate New York winter. . . . We have done our bits as agents of the state, done what we legally can. Still, I can't get him out of my mind. The tiny shards I know of his fractured and bruised experience overwhelm me with questions about what I'm doing as a teacher. (p. 4)

Weaving students' lives into our literacy teaching allows us to know them at
a deeper, more personal level, and this insight can lead to mutual relationships
of love and care. Loving, however, can be difficult; it requires unwavering
faith, fortitude, and a willingness to be vulnerable. A commitment to transformation, however, demands that we show students how to care by modeling and entering into a relationship of troth—a relationship that is necessary
for substantive change, and that is grounded in a moral vision.

## Dialogue

Spears-Bunton (1996) writes: "it is difficult to have respect and compassion
for the human spirit clothed differently from ourselves without knowledge of
the 'Other's' song, in his/her own voice" (p. 57). Classrooms must be places
where students and teachers can learn about the "Other's song" through a
process of mutual inquiry; where they can feel free to express themselves and
to take risks; where they can engage in open dialogue. They must be places
where all students can contribute to a culture of compassion and care and to
the ongoing narrative of the classroom through sharing their stories, confronting their fears, and revealing their passions.

As discussed in chapter 4, dialogue is characterized by the free and reciprocal exchange of ideas whereby students' thoughts and opinions are actively
solicited. Differing points of view are welcomed and become sources for collaborative inquiry, and students are encouraged to consider diverse perspectives in the rational pursuit of knowledge. It was suggested that open dialogue is inherently democratic in that it allows multiple voices to be heard
and considers disparate views in the process of deliberation. Here, this notion of dialogue is being extended to incorporate the subjective dimension of
knowledge—that dimension that takes us beyond scientific rationalism and
focuses on our human connectedness. Dialogue that nurtures a culture of
compassion and care is rooted in a holistic view of self that perceives the act
of human knowing as more than objective investigation and analytical reasoning. It is a view that acknowledges nonrational forms of human consciousness, that understands our interconnectedness with others and with
the universe, and that seeks to exploit this interconnectedness in order to
counter ecological destruction, social injustice, and human suffering (J.
Miller 1993). That is, it is a dialogue that emerges not from rational inquiry,
but from agape.

We engage in dialogue with others when we share not only our thoughts,
but also our feelings—when we communicate not only through our minds,
but through our hearts and souls. It is this type of dialogue that is required
for entering into relationship with others and for forging a genuine community of care. Parker Palmer writes that

As the dialogue goes on, a larger truth is revealed, a truth that is not only within us but *between* us. It is the truth that we are not autonomous agents, each with a private world, but are in community with each other. Community begins to emerge as we seek our inward nature. But it can grow only as we realize that our created nature calls us into obedient relationship with each other and all that we know; it can grow only as our inward response finds outward manifestations in relationships of dialogue and troth. (1993, pp. 90–91)

In revealing ourselves to others through dialogue, we enter into a community of truth, and within this community, we come to know ourselves.

Elementary teacher Bob Peterson creates this type of community in his classroom through discussing emotionally charged issues with his students. To illustrate, on one occasion he shared a photograph from the *New York Times* taken after a snowstorm that depicted "piles of snow-covered blankets and cardboard on park benches near the White House." Initially the children thought that the picture displayed piles of trash. When Peterson revealed that the piles were actually homeless people covered by snow, his students became angry. Peterson reports that the ensuing discussion "ranged from their own experiences seeing homeless people in the community to suggestions of what should be done by the president" (1994, p. 35). Their dialogue prompted one student to write the following poem:

> I walk to the park
> I see homeless people laying
> on a bench I feel sad
> to see people sleeping outside
> nowhere to go I felt
> to help them let them stay
> in a hotel
> give them things
> until they get
> a job and
> a house to stay
> and let them
> pay me back
> with their love.
>             (Jade Williams,
>               "Homeless")

Dialogue can emerge from a picture or photograph, a poem, a song, a selection from a student's writing journal, or a common experience with literature.

One of the most important ways for developing a community of care is to encourage students to give genuine responses to one another's writing. Several years ago, as part of a research project, I had the privilege of participating in a second grade classroom in eastern Kentucky with a teacher, "Karen," who used storytelling as her primary method of literacy instruction. During an ensuing interview, Karen described the effects of storytelling in her classroom:

> They will laugh out loud listening to somebody's funny story. They will shed tears and weep when a child talks about a pet that died or somebody that's left them. They experience every conceivable emotion. It could be feelings of love and devotion, all those very important values that a child needs in order to base a good sense of self, are all in those stories that they tell. And when they share those stories with each other, they get to know each other. And when you waste all that time on the basal reader every week, the children don't really get acquainted except on the surface. They don't learn admiration for each other. My children hug and pet on each other. I don't know if you noticed that today, but they reinforce and brag on each other. This isn't something that I've taught them. It just comes from the sharing of their souls. (Powell 1996, p. 12)

We can also encourage dialogue by allowing students to respond to literature in personal ways. When students have ownership in literature discussions, such as when they participate in student-led "literature circles," their dialogue is often richly meaningful, as they speak from their own personal experiences and support and extend the contributions of others in the group.[3] Short, Harste, and Burke (1996) describe the discussion of one group of fifth grade students as they shared their responses to the book *Baseball Saved Us* by Mochizuki (1993), a tale about a young Japanese American boy in an internment camp during World War II:

> John commented that, "people didn't like him because of his color, but the teammates just tried to help him." His comment reminded Tino of his experiences with baseball, "Like when we play, we try to make our smaller players feel good." The boys went on to talk about the guard in the story which Tino connected to his feelings of "I can't believe I did it" when he hit a home run in front of his dad. Ruben talked about being new, "I had to prove myself and that's when they started liking me," as he tried to understand how the boy felt when he was taunted at games. John pulled from his experiences as a Tohono O'odham to comment, "It's like a comparison. Like some people don't like blacks and Mexicans don't like whites sometimes. The white kids in the book, they're saying that they're better than him." "He didn't do nothing at all," Rudy commented, "but they thought that they (Japanese Americans) were gonna do something bad so they might as well put 'em in camps." (pp. 206–07)

The children in this discussion are doing more than sharing their thoughts and opinions. They are entering into the lives of the characters, making connections, and expanding their understanding of the human experience.

Dialogue need not be oral but can take place on paper through journaling. Nancie Atwell (1987) describes her use of dialogue journals in the middle school, which are used as vehicles for students to respond to literature either with one another or with the teacher. Peterson (1994) describes the use of double entry journals whereby students copy interesting sentences from a book they are reading on the left side of the page, and on the right side they write how it reminds them of something in their own lives. In all of these activities, the dialogue that occurs is not just rational and impersonal but, rather, can be affective and personal; it becomes an opportunity for students to share their souls.

*Practice*

Inviting students to give genuine and personal responses to one another's stories and to the stories of published authors not only engages students in dialogue, but it also enables them to practice an ethic of care. Such environments encourage students to contribute to the social, cognitive, and affective growth of their peers within a supportive collaborative community (e.g., Zaragoza 1997). An experience from my own teaching might serve as a useful illustration. I often model for my students the power of literature by reading excerpts from various literary works and asking them to respond in a personal way. For instance, in one particular graduate class, I read Shel Silverstein's poem "The Little Boy and the Old Man" (1981, p. 95), a profoundly moving verse that touches on the problems experienced by the very young and the very old. I then asked my students to respond to the poem through writing. The room was silent as they wrote down their thoughts. Later, as we shared our responses, tears flowed freely as students talked about how the poem reminded them of personal experiences with aging and death. Later that week, one of the teachers in the class chose to repeat this activity with her primary students. Many of the reactions of these eight-year-old children reveal remarkable sensitivity to the message of the text:

I thot that prer [poem] is funy. I now how he feols a lot of times I feol like that. He mit of benn por [poor]. (Levi)

I feel as if peple don't pay attintion to some peple because they are ether real old or because they are poor. The chiled in this poem probily feels he is being left out. (LeeAnn)

I thank the Mane [man] and the boy is nies [nice]. It macks me feil sade [sad]. and I baet it max them feile sad to. (Brandy)

I thak the little boy was right about the grownops wont lisin [listen] I tank the tow [two] pepol shoo [should] be frinds. (Scott)

I really liked the poem because it tells how they felt and I think the little old man felt very cared for then because he had someone to talk to. I think the little boy would feel good about having someone around for him to tell something to. The little old man kind of reminds me of my grandfather. (Ashley)

I intentionally select literature that will provoke an emotional response from my students and that will touch them at a personal level. For example, I occasionally read an excerpt from Maya Angelou's *I Know Why the Caged Bird Sings* (1969) describing her sense of humiliation resulting from the callous words of a local White politician who spoke at her graduation ceremony. This particular text often elicits a rich discussion about racism and the many manifestations of man's inhumanity. A text I have used with elementary teachers is Sherry Garland's *The Lotus Seed* (1993). This book tells the story of a young woman who escaped from Vietnam carrying only the seed of the lotus flower, which was to become her most valued possession. After reading the book aloud, I then ask students to write about their own personal treasures. Their responses not only help them to empathize with the character in the text, but they also reveal how our most precious possessions are not necessarily those that have material value, but rather those that represent significant relationships in our lives.

I have found that from such discussions, we learn a great deal about one another and come to value our common humanness. There is a sense of connectedness that emerges as a result of the sharing of one's personal responses to literature, both with the author and with one another. We come to see that we all experience pain, joy, despair—that we are all a part of the human experience.

Students also practice the ethic of care when they share their own stories within a caring classroom community. Stories connect us by revealing our hidden thoughts and fears, by "pushing back the darkness and binding us together into a community" (Calkins and Harwayne 1991, p. 106). In their book *Living Between the Lines,* Calkins and Harwayne (1991) describe the effects of one child's moving account of her brother's illness on the other students. Her story shows the power of language to cross cultural boundaries and reveal our interconnectedness.

> Dark-eyed Yolanda looked up only once from her paper. Watching, one felt that if she looked again into the eyes of her listeners, she would not be able to hold back her tears. And so she continued, quietly sharing the story of her little brother's debilitating disease, which she said is slowly distorting his features, turning him bit by bit into a freak. The doctor had given Yolanda's parents a photograph showing the full horror of what the boy would become, and recently Yolanda's cousin, in an act of anger, got hold of the photograph and showed it to the boy, taunting him with it.
>
> When Yolanda finished reading, a "stillness greatened" in the room. Then, in quiet voices, the children and their teacher, Pazcual Villaronga, began telling their own stories in response. One child spoke of how she sometimes looks in the mirror and sees in her mind a picture of what she's becoming. Another added that she sometimes feels that she's changing into a freak, too, only it's not her looks that are changing but her feelings. A tiny boy with huge brown eyes talked with

enormous empathy about how the cousin probably didn't mean to be so hurtful, and the boy said he is sometimes jealous of his little brother who gets attention because he has asthma. "What do you do with feelings like these?" the children asked themselves.

As Yolanda heard her friends empathizing with "the cousin," tears streamed down her face. When I watch moments such as this, I cannot help but think, "God, do we need stories." Stories can change the world. (p. 105)

It is the notion that stories can change the world that we must pass on to our students—not just some stories, but *their* stories. Like the teachers from South Africa, the world must hear their voices. Within a nurturing environment, narrative unites us into a caring community, it evokes compassion, it enriches our lives. By allowing students to become personally connected to the stories they read, write, and hear, they learn the power of narrative for transformation.

## Confirmation

When we offer confirmation, we affirm the worth of every individual. We send the message that they are valued and that their lives are significant despite their inadequacies. Yolanda's cousin was shown confirmation when his imperfections were forgiven and his underlying goodness was validated. Confirmation is also demonstrated in the following poem written by a high school senior about her relationship with her mother:

> For all the times you yelled
> and all the times you screamed
> I forgive you.
>
> For all the nights we had breakfast
> for dinner and dinner for breakfast
> I forgive you.
>
> For all the times I felt you were
> pushing my daddy away
> I forgive you.
>
> For all the times we ran away
> and came back,
> For all the times that we packed
> and unpacked,
>
> For all the friends I've lost
> and all the schools I've seen,
>
> For all the times
> I was the new kid on the scene,
> I forgive you.

For all the punishments
and all the lies
all the reasons
and the why's
All the maybe's
and all the okay's
I forgive you, Mommie,
for all the long days.
(Tanya Park,
"Forgiving My Mother,"
in *Rites of Passage,* 1994–95)

Confirmation occurs when the worth of every individual is continuously validated by other members of the group. Within such communities of care, there emerges an unspoken allegiance to one another; individuals become joined in communion, unified through compassion and human understanding. Randy Bomer (1995) recounts an experience in one of his senior English classes that illustrates this sense of mutual commitment that results in confirmation:

A member of their class, Joseph, had died four years earlier in a car accident. When Brian read aloud his memoir about Joseph, who'd been Brian's best friend, most of the class cried. Their tears seemed to be prompted by more than loss. It seemed important for them to show one another that, even after all this time had gone by and they'd all grown up so much, Joseph was *still* important to them all, they *still* missed him, they hadn't forgotten. Through their tears they were sharing not only their grief but their sense of community and their commitment to old friends. (p. 133)

Confirmation can only occur within an environment where students feel valued and affirmed, and where they are encouraged to demonstrate an ethic of care in their relations with one another.

One way to encourage confirmation is to challenge students to confront their own insensitivities and inadequacies. Teacher educator Suzanne SooHoo describes a situation in her college classroom that involved a learning disabled adult who "was prone to make socially inappropriate comments in class." On one particular night his monopolization of the class discussion was particularly irritating. After class, three students approached him and informed him that they felt his behavior was rude and tactless; later, they complained to SooHoo that "he doesn't belong here, he doesn't fit" and requested that she remove him from the class. SooHoo explains that she decided to turn their negative reactions into a "teachable moment" about teaching in a pluralistic classroom:

The following week I gave students a case study written by an elementary principal, a regular education, and a special education teacher describing a dilemma regarding the mainstreaming efforts of a special education student. The case focused on a young boy's difficulty in assuming regular education expectations and the regular education teacher's difficulty in adjusting her standards. Students volunteered to role-play the case study. Classmates watched their peers seek strategies requiring integration and instructional appropriateness, social acceptance, empathy, and compassion.

Following the simulation, public self-disclosures of discomfort at addressing student differences were made. "Why is it our first instinct is to exile any student that deviates from the social norms?" we asked ourselves. "Why do we not gravitate to those who are different in an attempt to understand them better?" (SooHoo and Wilson 1994, pp. 167–68)

SooHoo reports that this simulation experience helped students to understand their own discriminatory practices in her classroom, and they subsequently confirmed the problematic student's presence by "trying hard to appreciate him" and to understand his differences. Further, an examination of their own cultural biases led the students to an investigation of the hegemonic forces in society and schooling: patriarchy, bureaucracy, and the transmission model of learning.

Communities of compassion and care evolve naturally from classrooms that provide for collaborative dialogue, student voice, and mutual inquiry. We cannot make our students care; rather, we need to establish environments of reciprocal trust and regard that facilitate such relationships—that help students value others within the community and celebrate the richness of our diversity. We must also model caring relationships with our students and affirm their unique abilities and insights, validating their worth as individuals and revealing their capacities for greatness. Because schooled literacy is based upon a scientific, technicist rationality that legitimates only objective ways of knowing and denies our subjective experience, it can never be used to attain a nurturing and caring community. This aim can only be realized through a literacy that celebrates agape, and that provides opportunities for students to practice relations of care.

## WHOLE LANGUAGE AND TRANSFORMATIVE PEDAGOGY

Many of the pedagogical practices presented in this chapter evolve from a whole language conception of literacy and language. Therefore, I would be remiss if I did not examine whole language pedagogy and its relationship to a more critical, transformative literacy. Indeed, there is much in whole language teaching that is potentially emancipatory (Edelsky 1991). Whole language theory suggests that literacy is both a psychological process and a social construction; that is, oral and written texts are used to create meaning within particular social contexts. Thus, whole language endorses authentic, purposeful uses of language in which the language user has a certain amount of control over the linguistic event (i.e., students are positioned as subjects rather than as objects). Instruction based upon whole language theory centers around the acquisition and conveyance of meaning; hence, skills and strategies required for meaningful communication are taught within the context of actual reading and writing. Such instruction can be contrasted with exercises, which are solely used for the purposes of instruction or evaluation.

Edelsky (1991) argues (as I do throughout this book) that skills-based instruction—which gives the semblance of being neutral—actually serves to obscure the gatekeeping function of language instruction in schools. Children who have the linguistic capital to succeed—who know how to play the "reading-exercise game" and are familiar with the norms for "doing school" (p. 71), are more likely to succeed than nonmainstream students. Whole language–based instruction, on the other hand, legitimizes students' language and views all students as competent language users. Essentially, whole language pedagogy acknowledges that students come to school with legitimate language and experiences and builds upon their linguistic abilities through meaningful reading and writing tasks.

In the sense that whole language validates students' cultural knowledge and linguistic abilities and positions students as subjects, it is potentially liberatory. Whole language theory has done much to move us beyond a technicist notion of reading and writing instruction toward a more humane, child-centered perspective that begins with a consideration of students' strengths, interests, and experiences. It has done much to democratize our classrooms and teaching methods, to establish communities of learners, and to empower teachers. It has done much to change our conceptions of language assessment, from testing isolated skills to endorsing more authentic means for determining students' knowledge of written language. Nevertheless, it is important to acknowledge that whole language is essentially a linguistic theory—a theory that can inform us on questions relating to curriculum integration, methodology, language use, and accountability. What is lacking is a larger philosophical framework that examines more fundamental questions, such as "Why teach language?" and "What are schools for?" (Miller 1992; White 1991). Thus, while whole language may indeed be liberating for individual students, it need not be transformative. Liberation provides for individual escape; transformation requires social commitment. To be transformative, literacy instruction must challenge taken-for-granted assumptions about social, economic, and political inequities in our society.

What I am arguing here is that if language instruction is to be potentially transformative, then we must begin to have a shift in paradigms. Whole language versus skills debates continue to be framed within a scientific/technocratic paradigm whereby academic achievement is primary. As I argue elsewhere (Powell 1992), we must reinvent our goals for language instruction, and these goals must be linked to a democratic vision—one that is grounded in equity, compassion, and human understanding. These are fundamentally moral issues that require that we move beyond rational/technicist thinking—thinking that is constrained by the need for educational accountability within a so-called nation at risk—and address the larger concerns facing our national and global society.

What I am also suggesting is that whole language educators and critical theorists would benefit from an alliance that advocates a literacy that is both politicized and holistic. A radical literacy that engages us only in political debate without considering the ultimate ramifications of that debate for individuals and for society is essentially irresponsible. On the other hand, a literacy that is progressive yet focuses primarily on individual empowerment is limited in its capacity to affect substantive social change. What is needed is a critical literacy that links our "moral and spiritual consciousness, and society and the individual" (Purpel 1993, p. 90), a literacy that goes beyond rational constructions of hegemony and power and "explores the dialectical relationship between the worlds of subjective experience and the social world" (Kesson 1993, p. 93).

Holistic theory informs methodology; critical theory infuses methodology with political force. Holistic theory considers the wholeness of the human experience—social, cultural, cognitive, physical, affective, spiritual; critical theory demystifies the ways that differences in the human experience have been used to privilege and oppress.[4] Holistic theory leads to classrooms that affirm and nurture the linguistic, cognitive, and spiritual development of each child; critical theory directs students' development toward transformative versus solely individualistic ends. A literacy that is informed by both holistic and critical theory is one that is both child-centered and socially liberating, that enhances both our sense of individual worth and our collective consciousness, and that nourishes relationships of mutual care while compelling us to work for a more just and compassionate society. Surely, a literacy that is both critical and holistic will go far toward realizing a moral, democratic vision.

## CONCLUSION

In the preceding pages, I suggest that the transformative potential of a critical, proper literacy will be diminished unless it is mitigated by an ethic of compassion and care. Our vision for transformation must be a moral one—one that is driven by a goal of equity and that nurtures a collective social consciousness. A moral vision can never be realized through individual liberation but only becomes possible when it is grounded in agape, in a love for all humankind that transcends our personal aspirations and desires.

It is not customary to talk about agape in academic circles. Such words are thought to lack objectivity and scientific rigor, bordering on the subjective mysticism of earlier eras that scientific rationalism sought to replace. Yet it is precisely a discussion of love, or agape, that has been missing from the writings of many literacy theorists, and I would argue that this absence is problematic. Love must be the motivating force behind empowerment, not personal advancement or social adjustment; for it is love, and not a quest for power, that helps us to define our vision and that compels us to work for the common good. It challenges us to go beyond self-servitude and create a community that is characterized by sacrificial action and ethical practice. Unless it is motivated by love, a critical pedagogy has the potential to further divide us.

The reality is that our liberatory projects are often merely self-serving itineraries that masquerade as a quest for freedom and justice for all, and that thereby make a mockery of the goal of equity. Our emancipatory aims, inevitably conceived from our own limited experiences, often conceal and make us oblivious to our own oppressive actions. Hence, bell hooks (1994) admonishes White feminists to look at the ways that they have silenced the voices of Black women, and Cornel West (1993) exposes the ways that Black males have oppressed Black women and Jews. Unless we recognize and acknowledge how we also marginalize by privileging our own agendas rather than forging collective alliances, then genuine, liberatory transformation cannot occur. Nel Noddings reminds us that we all have the potential to do harm:

> Schools today do try to teach something about other cultures, and they often try to promote global awareness. But I am not talking about abstract learning that can dissipate immediately in a crisis. I am talking about an understanding of self and other that recognizes with a heavy heart that we are all vulnerable to error and to evil. I am concerned with reducing the tendency to project evil onto others not only to exteriorize and then destroy it, but also to deny its presence in ourselves. (1992, p. 54)

A commitment to illumination demands that those of us who claim to be critical educators make our own agendas objects of critique, and that we examine the motivations behind our quest for empowerment. We must acknowledge that we, too, are ideologically situated, and that we have multiple subjectivities that can place us simultaneously within spaces of privilege and marginalization.

Beyond this, we must acknowledge that our own beliefs as critical theorists have been shaped by a Cartesian worldview that privileges rational inquiry over other ways of knowing. We must recognize that there are other ways of seeing the world and our places within it that are equally valid and that can generate alternative visions and creative insights. These different ways of knowing can lead us into the subjective domain, a domain that is characterized by spiritual connectedness and relationships of care. When we are motivated by a love of humankind, questions of who are the oppressors and who are the oppressed tend to take on less significance. More significant are questions that ask *how* we oppress, through our unexamined values and assumptions.

Some would say that a vision that is motivated by love is utopian and can never be attained. They may be right. Certainly, we have never experienced such a world. Yet I would respond by saying that a world without a vision is a world without direction, purpose, or meaning. Indeed, this is very much the world we now inhabit. Visions have never been realized by fatalism, for fatalism denies our ability to be inspired by forces beyond our narcissistic desires, to be governed by faith, to be driven by compassion. In essence, fatalism denies our capacity to be fully human. Cornel West (1993) states that

> In these downbeat times, we need as much hope and courage as we do vision and analysis; we must accent the best of each other even as we point out the vicious effects of our racial divide and the pernicious consequences of our maldistribution of wealth and power. We simply cannot enter the twenty-first century at each other's throats, even as we acknowledge the weighty forces of racism, patriarchy, economic inequality, homophobia, and ecological abuse on our necks. We are at a crucial crossroad in the history of this nation—and we either hang together by combating these forces that divide and degrade us or we hang separately. Do we have the intelligence, humor, imagination, courage, tolerance, love, respect, and will to meet the challenge? Time will tell. None of us alone can save the nation or world. But each of us can make a positive difference if we commit ourselves to do so. (p. 159)

The problems of our society and world cry out for a prophetic voice, and as educators who touch present and future lives, we must contribute to that voice. We must establish aims that call for a better society—one that is grounded in equity and is characterized by compassion and care. We must be willing to engage in moral practice by becoming a part of the struggle to end oppression and to renew a sense of hope for future generations. We must nurture a collective and critical social consciousness and establish a community that is willing to act on its democratic principles and moral ideals. Certainly, educators alone cannot change the status quo. But we must try, for the world will not be moved through our silence.

## NOTES

1. Cultural authenticity is a critical factor in selecting multicultural/multiethnic books. For criteria to use in screening books for selection, see Bishop (1992), Banks (1994), and Day (1994). For listings of suggested books to use at various grade levels, see Harris (1992), Oliver (1994), Day (1994), and Willis (1998). Also recommended are *Through Indian Eyes: The Native Experience in Books for Children* edited by Beverly

Slapin and Doris Seale (1992), and *Roots and Branches: A Resource of Native American Literature* by Dorothea M. Susag (1998), both excellent resources for determining the appropriateness of various books on the Native American experience.

2. The names Karen Owsley and Bill McLean are pseudonymns used in a dissertation study.

3. It is beyond the scope of this book to describe various literacy instructional methods in depth. Readers are encouraged to consult the sources that are cited for a description of how these methods can be implemented in the classroom. For another excellent resource on using student-led literature discussion groups in classrooms, see Routman (1994).

4. For a comprehensive discussion of holistic education, see R. Miller (1992).

# Afterword: One Teacher's Journey

I end this book with a story. The words are those of Carol Stumbo, a high school English teacher from the Appalachian mountains of eastern Kentucky ("Focus" 1987). Her school is located in one of the most impoverished counties of the United States, in a region that has few opportunities for upward mobility and has been plagued for generations by a sense of hopelessness and despair.

Several years ago, Stumbo made the decision to abandon schooled literacy—a literacy that tended to alienate her students and to perpetuate passivity and dependency—and to initiate a more critical, emancipatory literacy. She subsequently transformed her English classroom into a magazine publishing studio. Her students interviewed persons in the community, transcribed their audiotapes, and developed articles for their magazine, *Mantrip* (Stumbo 1989).

The following reflections were written to the editor of *Hands-On,* a publication of Foxfire Fund Inc. (the forerunner to their current publication, *The Active Learner: A Foxfire Journal for Teachers*), during Stumbo's first two years as a transformative educator. Her words are a powerful testimony to the effects that a critical literacy can have on teachers, students, and communities.

September, 1985
I pushed back the chairs . . . and listened to my students at the beginning of the year and it has changed everything for me and for them. I listened to them today as they reported on what they have discovered in their conversations with people in the community and I watched their faces, and most of the anger, the sullen dislike of school, is not there. . . . Sometimes I realize how far I am in this class away from what I was doing last year and it scares me a little—not being sure of exactly where I am headed or how things will go the next day in class. Much of that depends on the kids. . . . I know now that I am going to be able to reach the

point this year where we can address some of the problems of our area on a higher level. That is going to come.

November, 1985
If you could hear some of these stories, especially from the miners. Some can't finish them because their voices start breaking up and the kids wait on them—and the kids come away different.

April, 1986
Reluctantly, my students and I will be deep into the textbook for English literature soon and the magazine will be a memory. . . . The kids were so scared when we started working in the literature book, afraid of English history and Beowulf and Chaucer. They expressed that fear to me and so we have worked on the problems that they have with the material. I feel a bond, as if it is only another problem that we have to work out just like we did on the magazine. We are working on the problems together. . . . The students are able to understand oral history, poets who memorized long epics or poems, because of the work on the magazine. One of them asked me the other day why he needed to learn about something that happened such a long time ago and all I had to do to make him understand was to pull out some of the information that we had learned during the interviews about transportation and mining and remind him of why he needed to know that in order to understand the present in eastern Kentucky.

May, 1986
Two nights ago, we had a celebration for all those involved with the magazine. It was eerie listening to the people that we had interviewed for the magazine, talking about the project. They spoke about the need for involvement in the school, about what they could offer from their lives to young people, about taking pride in their community again, and even the need for independence—the need to work for things and stop being so passive, depending on others. It just struck me so strongly as I stood in the back of the cafeteria listening to them, that here is the answer for us. As I stood looking around at the facilities, one of the most run-down schools in the county, a county dominated by politics and greed and the power of a few, that there was a force in these people that could make a difference and that we had made some kind of beginning. . . . I feel the rightness and the strength of what we are trying to do.

October, 1986
We have had a rough time with four boys in the class. We have just had to keep proving to them that we meant what we said about treating them with respect and our persistence and the passage of time did that with three of them. I really thought I had lost with one of them though. Last week I told him to take some time and think about whether he wanted to work with us. He had driven me to the point of exasperation—so angry, so hard. I asked him to spend some time away from us thinking about it. He came back this week and told us that he had missed the class so much he couldn't stand it. He's back and he's different—no

problems. I think it just took him all these weeks to accept the fact that we weren't playing the game that goes on in the rest of the school. Already this year, rocks have been thrown through the windows in the offices and several classrooms, one of the boys' bathrooms has been locked because sinks have been torn off the walls and holes rammed into the doors. Things go untouched in our classroom. How that can be in the midst of all this other is sometimes incredible. But Robin, who has been beaten down all his life, has a place for one hour during the day where he does not have to fight, and that is enough for me. ("Focus" 1987, pp. 5–7)

Our society suffers from enormous social and economic problems, problems that demand a moral imagination that is embedded within an ethic of caring. These problems will not be addressed through our silence but rather will only be solved by teachers and students like these, who have begun to transcend their former limited visions resulting from their own school experiences and articulate an alternate rationality. Teachers must begin to see education as inherently political and schools as political institutions. They must begin to question why they are educating, and whose purposes it ultimately serves. For it is only in seeking answers to these questions that teachers will come to understand the need for a critical, proper literacy for both themselves and their students—one that will allow them to interrogate their own reality and will empower them to work for change.

# References

Allington, R. L. 1991. Children who find learning to read difficult: School responses to diversity. In E. H. Hiebert (ed.), *Literacy for a diverse society: Perspectives, practices, and policies* (pp. 237–52). New York: Teachers College Press.

Anderson, R. C., E. H. Hiebert, J. A. Scott, and A. G. Wilkinson. 1985. *Becoming a nation of readers: The report of the Commission on Reading.* Washington, D.C.: U.S. Department of Education.

Angelou, M. 1969. *I know why the caged bird sings.* New York: Bantam Books.

Anyon, J. 1983. Workers, labor and economic history, and textbook content. In M. W. Apple and L. Weis (eds.), *Ideology and practice in schooling* (pp. 37–60). Philadelphia: Temple University Press.

Apple, M. W. 1982. *Education and power.* Boston: Routledge and Kegan Paul.

———. 1983. Curricular form and the logic of technical control. In M. W. Apple and L. Weis (eds.), *Ideology and practice in schooling* (pp. 143–65). Philadelphia: Temple University Press.

———. 1988. *Teachers and texts: A political economy of class and gender relations in education.* New York: Routledge and Kegan Paul.

———. 1993a. Between moral regulation and democracy: The cultural contradictions of the text. In C. Lankshear and P. L. McLaren (eds.), *Critical literacy: Politics, praxis, and the postmodern* (pp. 193–216). Albany: SUNY Press.

———. 1993b. *Official knowledge: Democratic education in a conservative age.* New York: Routledge.

Apple, M. W., and S. Jungck. 1993. Whose curriculum is this anyway? In M. W. Apple, *Official knowledge: Democratic education in a conservative age* (pp. 118–42). New York: Routledge.

Applebee, A. N. 1989. *A study of book-length works taught in high school English courses.* Albany, N.Y.: Center for the Learning and Teaching of Literature.

———. 1991. Literature: Whose heritage? In E. H. Hiebert (ed.), *Literacy for a diverse society: Perspectives, practices, and policies* (pp. 228–36). New York: Teachers College Press.

Arblaster, A. 1987. *Democracy.* Minneapolis: University of Minnesota Press.

Aronowitz, S., and H. A. Giroux. 1985. *Education under siege: The conservative, liberal and radical debate over schooling.* South Hadley, Mass.: Bergin and Garvey.

Atwell, N. 1987. *In the middle: Writing, reading, and learning with adolescents.* Portsmouth, N.H.: Heinemann.

Au, K. H. 1993. *Literacy instruction in multicultural settings.* Fort Worth, Tex.: Harcourt Brace Jovanovich.

Banks, J. A. 1991. A curriculum for empowerment, action, and change. In C. E. Sleeter (ed.), *Empowerment through multicultural education* (pp. 125–41). Albany: SUNY Press.

————. 1994. *An introduction to multicultural education.* Boston: Allyn and Bacon.

————. 1997. *Educating citizens in a multicultural society.* New York: Teachers College Press.

Barber, B. R. 1984. *Strong democracy: Participatory politics for a new age.* Berkeley: University of California Press.

————. 1992. *An aristocracy of everyone: The politics of education and the future of America.* New York: Ballantine Books.

Bellah, R. N., R. Madsen, W. M. Sullivan, A. Swidler, and S. M. Tipton. 1985. *Habits of the heart: Individualism and commitment in American life.* New York: Harper and Row.

Bennett, K. P. 1991. Doing school in an urban Appalachian first grade. In C. E. Sleeter (ed.), *Empowerment through multicultural education* (pp. 27–47). Albany: SUNY Press.

Berg, I. 1971. *Education and jobs: The great training robbery.* Boston: Beacon Press.

Beyer, L. E., and D. P. Liston. 1996. *Curriculum in conflict: Social visions, educational agendas, and progressive school reform.* New York: Teachers College Press.

Bigelow, W. 1992. Inside the classroom: Social vision and critical pedagogy. In P. Shannon (ed.), *Becoming political: Readings and writings in the politics of literacy education* (pp. 72–82). Portsmouth, N.H.: Heinemann.

Bishop, R. S. 1992. Multicultural literature for children: Making informed choices. In V. J. Harris (ed.), *Teaching multicultural literature in grades K–8.* Norwood, Mass.: Christopher-Gordon.

Blake, B. E. 1997. *She say, he say: Urban girls write their lives.* Albany: SUNY Press.

Bloom, A. 1987. *The closing of the American mind.* New York: Simon and Schuster.

Bloome, D. 1987. Reading as a social process in a middle school classroom. In D. Bloome (ed.), *Literacy and schooling* (pp. 123–49). Norwood, N.J.: Ablex.

Bloome, D., and S. Nieto. 1992. Children's understandings of basal readers. In P. Shannon (ed.), *Becoming political: Readings and writings in the politics of literacy education* (pp. 83–93). Portsmouth, N.H.: Heinemann.

Boal, A. 1996. Keynote address. Pedagogy of the Oppressed Conference, Omaha, Nebr., March 21.

Bomer, R. 1995. *Time for meaning: Crafting literate lives in middle and high school.* Portsmouth, N.H.: Heinemann.

Bowers, C. A. 1988. *The cultural dimensions of educational computing: Understanding the non-neutrality of technology.* New York: Teachers College Press.

————. 1993. *Critical essays on education, modernity, and the recovery of the ecological imperative.* New York: Teachers College Press.

Bridges, D. 1988. *Education, democracy and discussion.* Lanham, Md.: University Press of America.

Brock, E., Q. Davis, Y. Levi, and C. Yoder (eds). 1994–95. *Rites of passage: A literary magazine.* Portland, Oreg.: Thomas Jefferson High School.

Brown, R. G. 1991. *Schools of thought: How the politics of literacy shape thinking in the classroom.* San Francisco: Jossey-Bass.

Callan, E. 1993. Democracy and schooling. In J. P. Portelli and S. Bailin (eds.), *Reason and values: New essays in philosophy of education* (pp. 151–70). Calgary, Alberta, Canada: Detselig Enterprises.

Calkins, L. M. 1986/1994. *The art of teaching writing.* Portsmouth, N.H.: Heinemann.

Calkins, L. M., and S. Harwayne. 1991. *Living between the lines.* Portsmouth, N.H.: Heinemann.

Castenell, L. A., Jr., and W. F. Pinar (eds.). 1993. *Understanding curriculum as racial text: Representations of identity and difference in education.* Albany: SUNY Press.

Cazden, C. B. 1988. *Classroom discourse: The language of teaching and learning.* Portsmouth, N.H.: Heinemann.

Cherryholmes, C. H. 1988. *Power and criticism: Poststructural investigations in education.* New York: Teachers College Press.

Children in Poverty. 1993. *Education Week* 13 (4), Sept. 29: 3.

Christensen, L. 1994. Whose standard? Teaching Standard English. In B. Bigelow, L. Christensen, S. Karp, B. Miner, and B. Peterson (eds.), *Rethinking our classrooms: Teaching for equity and justice* (pp. 142–45). Milwaukee, Wis.: Rethinking Schools, Ltd.

Christie, F. 1987. The morning news genre: Using a functional grammar to illuminate educational issues. *Australian Review of Applied Linguistics* 10: 182–98.

Clifford, G. J. 1984. Buch und lesen: Historical perspectives on literacy and schooling. *Review of Educational Research* 54: 472–500.

Cohen, B. 1990. *The long way home.* New York: Lothrop, Lee and Shepard.

Cohen, D. L. 1993. Half of Black, Hispanic children may be poor by 2010. *Education Week* (Nov. 3): 11.

Collins, J. 1989. Hegemonic practice: Literacy and standard language in public education. *Journal of Education* 171: 9–34.

Collins, J., and S. Michaels. 1986. Speaking and writing: Discourse strategies and the acquisition of literacy. In J. Cook-Gumperz (ed.), *The social construction of literacy* (pp. 207–22). Cambridge: Cambridge University Press.

Collison, M. 1994. Spanish for native speakers. *The Chronicle of Higher Education* XL (22), Feb. 2: A15–A16.

Cook-Gumperz, J. (ed.). 1986. *The social construction of literacy.* Cambridge: Cambridge University Press.

Cummins, J. 1986. Empowering minority students: A framework for intervention. *Harvard Educational Review* 56: 18–36.

Davidson, A. L. 1996. *Making and molding identity in schools: Student narratives on race, gender, and academic engagement.* Albany: SUNY Press.

Davis, Q. 1994–95. Ebony woman. In E. Brock, Q. Davis, G. Levi, and C. Yoder (eds.), *Rites of passage: A literary magazine* (p. 90). Portland, Oreg.: Thomas Jefferson High School.

Day, F. A. 1994. *Multicultural voices in contemporary literature: A resource for teachers*. Portsmouth, N.H.: Heinemann.

de Castell, S., and A. Luke. 1986. Models of literacy in North American schools: Social and historical conditions and consequences. In S. de Castell, A. Luke, and K. Egan (eds.), *Literacy, society, and schooling: A reader* (pp. 87–109). Cambridge: Cambridge University Press.

de Castell, S., A. Luke, and D. MacLennan. 1986. On defining literacy. In S. de Castell, A. Luke, and K. Egan (eds.), *Literacy, society, and schooling: A reader* (pp. 3–14). Cambridge: Cambridge University Press.

Delpit, L. 1988. The silenced dialogue: Power and pedagogy in educating other people's children. *Harvard Educational Review* 58: 280–98.

———. 1995. *Other people's children: Cultural conflict in the classroom*. New York: The New Press.

———. 1998. What should teachers do? Ebonics and culturally responsive instruction. In T. Perry and L. Delpit (eds.), *The real Ebonics debate* (pp. 17–26). Boston: Beacon Press.

Detlefsen, K. 1998. Diversity and the individual in Dewey's philosophy of democratic education. *Educational Theory* 48 (3): 309–29.

Dewey, J. 1916. *Democracy and education: An introduction to the philosophy of education*. New York: Macmillan.

Duffy, G. G. 1991. What counts in teacher education? Dilemmas in educating empowered teachers. In J. Zutell and S. McCormick (eds.), *Learner factors/teacher factors: Issues in literacy research and instruction* (pp. 1–18). Chicago: National Reading Conference.

Edelsky, C. 1991. *With literacy and justice for all: Rethinking the social in language and education*. Bristol, Pa.: Falmer Press, Taylor and Francis.

Eller, R. G. 1989a. *Teacher resistance and educational change: Toward a critical theory of literacy in Appalachia*. Unpublished dissertation, University of Kentucky, Lexington.

———. 1989b. Johnny can't talk, either: The perpetuation of the deficit theory in classrooms. *The Reading Teacher* 42 (9): 670–74.

Ellsworth, E. 1989. Why doesn't this feel empowering? Working through the repressive myths of critical pedagogy. *Harvard Educational Review* 59 (3): 297–324.

Erickson, F. 1984. School literacy, reasoning, and civility: An anthropologist's perspective. *Review of Educational Research* 54: 525–46.

———. 1987. Transformation and school success: The politics and culture of educational achievement. In E. Jacob and C. Jordan (eds.), *Explaining the school performance of minority students* [theme issue]. *Anthropology and Education Quarterly* 18: 335–56.

Facts on File. 1993. *Facts on file yearbook 1992: Vol. 52*. New York: Facts on File, Inc.

———. 1995. *Facts on file yearbook 1994: Vol. 54*. New York: Facts on File, Inc.

Fine, M. 1991. *Framing dropouts: Notes on the politics of an urban public high school*. Albany: SUNY Press.

Fiske, J. 1989. *Reading the popular*. Boston: Unwin Hyman.

Focus: A ride on the Mantrip. 1987. *Hands On* 8 (3): 4–13.

Fordham, S. 1991. Peer-proofing academic competition among Black adolescents:

"Acting White" Black American style. In C. E. Sleeter (ed.), *Empowerment through multicultural education* (pp. 69–93). Albany: SUNY Press.

Fox, P. 1973. *The slave dancer.* New York: Bantam Doubleday Day Publishing Group.

Freedman, S., J. Jackson and K. Boles. 1983. Teaching: An imperiled "profession." In L. S. Shulman and G. Sykes (eds.), *Handbook of teaching and policy* (pp. 261–99). New York: Longman.

Freire, P. 1970/1993. *Pedagogy of the oppressed.* New York: Continuum.

Freire, P., and D. Macedo. 1987. *Literacy: Reading the word and the world.* South Hadley, Mass.: Bergin and Garvey.

Garcia, E. 1994. *Understanding and meeting the challenge of student cultural diversity.* Boston: Houghton Mifflin.

Garland, S. 1993. *The lotus seed.* San Diego: Harcourt Brace and Co.

Gathercoal, F. 1993. *Judicious discipline.* 3d ed. San Francisco: Caddo Gap Press.

Gaughan, J. 1997. *Cultural reflections: Critical teaching and learning in the English classroom.* Portsmouth, N.H.: Boynton/Cook.

Gee, J. P. 1989. Literacy, discourse, and linguistics: Introduction [special issue]. *Journal of Education* 171: 5–17.

———. 1990. *Social linguistics and literacies: Ideology in discourses.* New York: Falmer Press.

———. 1992. What is literacy? In P. Shannon (ed.), *Becoming political: Readings and writings in the politics of literacy education* (pp. 21–28). Portsmouth, N.H.: Heinemann.

Gelb, S. A., and D. T. Mizokawa. 1986. Special education and social structure: The commonality of "exceptionality." *American Educational Research Journal* 23: 543–57.

Gelwick, R. 1977. *The way of discovery.* New York: Oxford University Press.

Gilmore, P. 1987. Sulking, stepping and tracking: The effects of attitude assessment on access to literacy. In D. Bloome (ed.), *Literacy and schooling* (pp. 98–120). Norwood, N.J.: Ablex.

———. 1992. "Gimme Room": School resistance, attitude, and access to literacy. In P. Shannon (ed.), *Becoming political: Readings and writings in the politics of literacy education* (pp. 113–27). Portsmouth, N.H.: Heinemann.

Giroux, H. A. 1988. *Teachers as intellectuals: Toward a critical pedagogy of learning.* South Hadley, Mass.: Bergin and Garvey.

———. 1992. Textual authority and the role of teachers as public intellectuals. In C. M. Hurlbert and S. Totten (eds.), *Social issues in the English classroom* (pp. 304–21). Urbana, Ill.: NCTE.

———. 1993. *Living dangerously: Multiculturalism and the politics of difference.* New York: Peter Lang.

Gitlin, A. 1983. School structure and teachers' work. In M. W. Apple and L. Weis (eds.), *Ideology and practice in schooling* (pp. 193–212). Philadelphia: Temple University Press.

Goldenberg, C. N. 1989. Making success a more common experience for children at risk of failure: Lessons from Hispanic first graders learning to read. In J. B. Allen and J. M. Mason (eds.), *Risk makers, risk takers, risk breakers: Reducing the risks for young literacy learners* (pp. 48–79). Portsmouth, N.H.: Heinemann.

Goodlad, J. 1984. *A place called school.* New York: McGraw-Hill.

Goody, J., and I. Watt. 1985. The consequences of literacy. In P. P. Giglioli (ed.), *Language and social context* (pp. 311–57). New York: Viking Penguin.

Graff, G. 1992. *Beyond the culture wars: How teaching the conflicts can revitalize American education.* New York: W. W. Norton.

Graff, H. J. 1987. *The labyrinths of literacy: Reflections on literacy past and present.* New York: Falmer Press.

Grant, L., and J. Rothenberg. 1986. The social enhancement of ability differences: Teacher-student interactions in first- and second-grade reading groups. *The Elementary School Journal* 87: 29–49.

Graves, D. H. 1994. *A fresh look at writing.* Portsmouth, N.H.: Heinemann.

Gray, W. S. 1956. *The teaching of reading and writing.* Paris: United Nations Educational, Scientific, and Cultural Organization (UNESCO).

*Great mountain tales.* 1989. Barbourville, Ky.: G. R. Hampton Elementary.

Greene, M. 1978. *Landscapes of learning.* New York: Teachers College Press.

Greenfield, E. 1988. *Nathanial talking.* New York: Black Butterfly Children's Books.

Gumperz, J. 1985. The speech community. In P. P. Giglioli (ed.), *Language and social context* (pp. 219–31). New York: Viking Penguin.

Gutmann, A. 1987. *Democratic education.* Princeton: Princeton University Press.

Halliday, M. A. K. 1985. *Spoken and written language.* Victoria: Deakin University.

Halliday, M. A. K., and R. Hasan. 1985. *Language, context, and text: Aspects of language in a social-semiotic perspective.* Victoria: Deakin University.

Harrington, H. L. 1993. The essence of technology and the education of teachers. *Journal of Teacher Education* 44: 5–15.

Harris, V. J. (ed.). 1992. *Teaching multicultural literature in grades K–8.* Norwood, Mass.: Christopher-Gordon Press.

Heap, J. L. 1988. Reading as rational action: Functioning and literacy in daily life. Paper presented at the meeting of the National Reading Conference, Tucson, Ariz., December.

Heath, S. B. 1983. *Ways with words: Language, life, and work in communities and classrooms.* Cambridge: Cambridge University Press.

Heflin, J. F. 1991. Demographics in the United States from now to the year 2000. In J. J. Harris III, C. A. Heid, D. G. Carter, Sr., and F. Brown (eds.), *Readings on the state of education in urban America* (pp. 57–66). Bloomington/Indianapolis: Indiana University, Center for Urban and Multicultural Education.

Helms, J. E. (ed.). 1993. *Black and white racial identity: Theory, research, and practice.* Westport, Conn.: Praeger.

Hiebert, E. H., and C. W. Fisher. 1991. Task and talk structures that foster literacy. In E. H. Hiebert (ed.), *Literacy for a diverse society: Perspectives, practices, and policies* (pp. 141–56). New York: Teachers College Press.

Hirsch, E. D., Jr. 1987. *Cultural literacy: What every American needs to know.* New York: Vintage Books.

Hollins, E. R., and K. Spencer. 1990. Restructuring schools for cultural inclusion: Changing the schooling process for African American youngsters. *Journal of Education* 172: 89–100.

Holt, M. 1993. The educational consequences of W. Edwards Deming. *Phi Delta Kappan* 74: 382–88.

hooks, b. 1994. *Teaching to transgress: Education as the practice of freedom*. New York: Routledge.

Horvath, B. M. 1977. Sociolinguistics and reading. In R. W. Shuy (ed.), *Linguistic theory: What can it say about reading?* (pp. 95–107). Newark, Del.: International Reading Association.

Hourigan, M. M. 1994. *Literacy as social exchange: Intersections of class, gender, and culture*. Albany: SUNY Press.

Houston, S. H. 1970. A reexamination of some assumptions about the language of the disadvantaged child. *Child Development* 41: 947–63.

Hull, G. 1993. Hearing other voices: A critical assessment of popular views on literacy and work. *Harvard Educational Review* 63: 20–49.

Hymes, D. 1986. Models of the interaction of language and social life. In J. J. Gumperz and D. Hymes (eds.), *Directions in sociolinguistics: The ethnography of communication* (pp. 35–71). New York: Basil Blackwell.

Jordan, J. 1988. Nobody mean more to me than you and the future life of Willie Jordan. *Harvard Educational Review* 58: 363–74.

Kane, J. 1993. Toward living knowledge: A Waldorf perspective. In R. Miller (ed.), *The renewal of meaning in education: Responses to the cultural and ecological crisis of our times* (pp. 111–28). Brandon, Vt.: Holistic Education Press.

Kaye, H. J., and D. B. Curtis, Jr. 1993. Education and democracy: Should the fact that we live in a democratic society make a difference in what our schools are like? In J. L. Kincheloe and S. R. Steinberg (eds.), *Thirteen questions: Reframing education's conversation* (pp. 123–39). New York: Peter Lang.

Keddie, N. 1971. Classroom knowledge. In M. F. D. Young (ed.), *Knowledge and control* (pp. 133–60). London: Collier-Macmillan.

Keesing, R. M. 1974. Theories of culture. In B. J. Siegel, A. R. Beals, and S. A. Tyler (eds.), *Annual reviews of anthropology* (vol. 3, pp. 73–97). Palo Alto, Calif.: Annual Reviews, Inc.

Kendrick, D. M. 1994. From caretaking to caregiving: Divergent perspectives upon teachers of the handicapped. In A. R. Prillaman, D. J. Eaker, and D. M. Kendrick (eds.), *The tapestry of caring: Education as nurturance* (pp. 15–31). Norwood, N.J.: Ablex.

Kesson, K. 1993. Critical theory and holistic education: Carrying on the conversation. In R. Miller (ed.), *The renewal of meaning in education: Responses to the cultural and ecological crises of our times* (pp. 92–110). Brandon, Vt.: Holistic Education Press.

Kincheloe, J. L. 1991. *Teachers as researchers: Qualitative inquiry as a path to empowerment*. New York: Falmer Press.

———. 1993. *Toward a critical politics of teacher thinking: Mapping the postmodern*. Westport, Conn.: Bergin and Garvey.

Knoblauch, C. H., and L. Brannon. 1993. *Critical teaching and the idea of literacy*. Portsmouth, N.H.: Heinemann.

Kohl, H. R. 1995. *"I won't learn from you": And other thoughts on creative maladjustment*. New York: The New Press.

Kohn, A. 1993. Choice for children: Why and how to let students decide. *Phi Delta Kappan* 75 (1): 8–20.

Labov, W. 1985. The logic of nonstandard English. In P. P. Giglioli (ed.), *Language and social context* (pp. 179–215). New York: Viking Penguin.

Lankshear, C., and M. Lawler. 1987. *Literacy, schooling and revolution*. Philadelphia: Falmer Press.

LeCompte, M. D., and K. B. deMarrais. 1992. The disempowering of empowerment: Out of the revolution and into the classroom. *Educational Foundations* 6: 5–31.

Luke, A. 1988. *Literacy, textbooks and ideology: Postwar literacy instruction and the mythology of Dick and Jane*. Philadelphia: Falmer Press.

Macedo, D. 1994. *Literacies of power: What Americans are not allowed to know*. Boulder, Colo.: Westview Press.

MacLeod, J. 1987. *Ain't no makin' it: Leveled aspirations in a low-income neighborhood*. Boulder, Colo.: Westview Press.

———. 1995. *Ain't no makin' it: Aspirations and attainment in a low-income neighborhood*. Boulder, Colo.: Westview Press.

McCarthy, C. 1988. Rethinking liberal and radical perspectives on racial inequality in schooling: Making the case for nonsynchrony. *Harvard Educational Review* 58: 256–79.

McCutcheon, G. 1988. Curriculum and the work of teachers. In L. E. Beyer and M. W. Apple (eds.), *The curriculum: Problems, politics, and possibilities* (pp. 191–203). Albany: SUNY Press.

McDermott, R. P. 1974. Achieving school failure: An anthropological approach to illiteracy and social stratification. In G. D. Spindler (ed.), *Education and cultural process: Toward an anthropology of education* (pp. 82–118). New York: Holt, Rinehart and Winston.

McIntosh, P. 1988. *White privilege and male privilege: A personal account of coming to see correspondences through work in women's studies* (Working Papers Series No. 189). Wellesley, Mass.: Wellesley College, Center for Research on Women.

McLaren, P. L. 1988. Culture or canon? Critical pedagogy and the politics of literacy. *Harvard Educational Review* 58: 213–34.

McLaren, P. L., and H. A. Giroux. 1997. Writing from the margins: Geographies of identity, pedagogy, and power. In P. McLaren (ed.), *Revolutionary multiculturalism: Pedagogies of dissent for the new millennium* (pp. 16–41). Boulder, Colo.: Westview Press.

McLaren, P. L., and C. Lankshear. 1993. Critical literacy and the postmodern turn. In C. Lankshear and P. L. McLaren (eds.), *Critical literacy: Politics, praxis, and the postmodern* (pp. 379–419). Albany: SUNY Press.

McNeil, L. M. 1988. *Contradictions of control: School structure and school knowledge*. New York: Routledge.

Melson, T. 1994–95. A box of our own. In E. Brock, Q. Davis, G. Levi, and C. Yoder (eds.), *Rites of passage: A literary magazine* (p. 3). Portland, Oreg.: Thomas Jefferson High School.

Miller, J. P. 1993. Worldviews, educational orientations, and holistic education. In R. Miller (ed.), *The renewal of meaning in education: Responses to the cultural and ecological crisis of our times* (pp. 53–67). Brandon, Vt.: Holistic Education Press.

Miller, R. 1992. *What are schools for? Holistic education in American culture*. Brandon, Vt.: Holistic Education Press.

Mochizuki, K. 1993. *Baseball saved us*. New York: Lee and Low.

Moll, L. C., and S. Diaz. 1987. Change as the goal of educational research. In E. Jacob and C. Jordan (eds.), *Explaining the school performance of minority students* [theme issue]. *Anthropology and Educational Quarterly* 18: 300–11.

Noddings, N. 1992. *The challenge to care in schools: An alternative approach to education.* New York: Teachers College Press.

———. 1995. Teaching themes of care. *Phi Delta Kappa* 76 (9): 675–79.

Oakes, J. 1985. *Keeping track: How schools structure inequality.* New Haven: Yale University Press.

O'Connor, S. 1996. *Will my name be shouted out?* New York: Simon and Schuster.

O'Connor, T. 1988. Cultural voice and strategies for multicultural education. Paper presented at the meeting of the American Educational Studies Association, Toronto, Canada, November.

Ogbu, J. 1987. Variability in minority school performance: A problem in search of an explanation. In E. Jacob and C. Jordan (eds.), *Explaining the school performance of minority students* [theme issue]. *Anthropology and Education Quarterly* 18: 312–34.

———. 1990. Literacy and schooling in subordinate cultures: The case of Black Americans. In K. Lomotey (ed.), *Going to school: The African-American experience* (pp. 113–31). Albany: SUNY Press.

Oliver, E. I. 1994. *Crossing the mainstream: Multicultural perspectives in teaching literature.* Urbana, Ill.: NCTE.

Opitz, M. F. (ed.) 1998. *Literacy instruction for culturally and linguistically diverse students.* Newark, Del.: International Reading Association.

Ortiz, F. I. 1988. Hispanic-American children's experiences in classrooms: A comparison between Hispanic and non-Hispanic children. In L. Weis (ed.), *Class, race, and gender in American education* (pp. 63–86). Albany: SUNY Press.

Pagano, J. L., and J. L. Miller. 1993. Women and education: In what ways does gender affect the educational process? In J. L. Kincheloe and S. R. Steinberg (eds.), *Thirteen questions: Reframing education's conversation* (pp. 141–58). New York: Peter Lang.

Palmer, P. J. 1983/1993. *To know as we are known: Education as a spiritual journey.* New York: HarperCollins.

Pang, V. O. 1991. Teaching children about social issues: Kidpower. In C. E. Sleeter (ed.), *Empowerment through multicultural education* (pp. 179–97). Albany: SUNY Press.

Pappas, C. C., B. Z. Kiefer, and L. S. Levstik. 1990. *An integrated language perspective in the elementary school.* White Plains, N.Y.: Longman.

Park, T. 1994–95. Forgiving my mother. In E. Brock, Q. Davis, G. Levi, and C. Yoder (eds.), *Rites of passage: A literary magazine* (p. 100). Portland, Oreg.: Thomas Jefferson High School.

Paterson, K. 1992. Tale of a reluctant dragon. In P. Shannon (ed.), *Becoming political: Readings and writings in the politics of literacy education* (pp. 53–59). Portsmouth, N.H.: Heinemann.

Perry, T., and L. Delpit (eds.). 1998. *The real Ebonics debate: Power, language, and the education of African-American children.* Boston: Beacon Press.

Perry, T., and J. W. Fraser (eds.). 1993. *Freedom's plow: Teaching in the multicultural classroom.* New York: Routledge.

Peterson, B. 1994. Teaching for social justice: One teacher's journey. In B. Bigelow,

L. Christensen, S. Karp, B. Miner, and B. Peterson (eds.), *Rethinking our class-rooms: Teaching for equity and justice* (pp. 30–33). Milwaukee: Rethinking Schools, Ltd.

Phillips, D. C. 1993. Incredulity about incredulity about value neutrality. *Educational Foundations* 7: 33–44.

Popkewitz, T. S. 1987. Ideology and social formation in teacher education. In T. S. Popkewitz (ed.), *Critical studies in teacher education: Its folklore, theory and practice.* New York: Falmer Press.

Powell, R. E. 1992. Goals for the language arts program: Toward a democratic vision. *Language Arts* 69 (5): 342–49.

————. 1996. Teachers as change agents: Countering hegemony through critical au-tobiography. Paper presented at the Pedagogy of the Oppressed Conference, Omaha, Nebr., March.

Purpel, D. E. 1989. *The moral and spiritual crisis in education.* Westport, Conn.: Bergin and Garvey.

————. 1993. Holistic education in a prophetic voice. In R. Miller (ed.), *The renewal of meaning in education: Responses to the cultural and ecological crisis of our times* (pp. 68–91). Brandon, Vt.: Holistic Education Press.

Reyhner, J. 1992. Plans for dropout prevention and special school support services for American Indian and Alaska Native students. In P. Cahape and C. B. Howley (eds.), *Indian nations at risk: Listening to the people* (pp. 42–46). Charleston, W. Va.: ERIC Clearinghouse on Rural Education and Small Schools.

Rist, R. C. 1970. Student social class and teacher expectations: The self-fulfilling prophecy in ghetto education. *Harvard Educational Review* 40: 411–51.

Rose, M. 1989. *Lives on the boundary.* New York: Penguin.

Roszak, T. 1986. *The cult of information: The folklore of computers and the true art of thinking.* New York: Pantheon.

Routman, R. 1994. *Invitations: Changing as teachers and learners K–12.* Portsmouth, N.H.: Heinemann.

Scholes, R. 1986. Aiming a canon at the curriculum. *Salmagundi* 72: 101–16.

Shannon, P. 1989. *Broken promises: Reading instruction in twentieth-century Amer-ica.* Granby, Mass.: Bergin and Garvey.

————. 1990. *The struggle to continue: Progressive reading instruction in the United States.* Portsmouth, N.H.: Heinemann.

————. 1998. *Reading poverty.* Portsmouth, N.H.: Heinemann.

————, (ed.). 1992. *Becoming political: Readings and writings in the politics of literacy education.* Portsmouth, N.H.: Heinemann.

Shapiro, S. 1990. *Between capitalism and democracy: Educational policy and the crisis of the welfare state.* New York: Bergin and Garvey.

Shor, I. 1992. *Empowering education: Critical teaching for social change.* Chicago: University of Chicago Press.

Shor, I., and P. Freire. 1987. *A pedagogy for liberation: Dialogues on transforming ed-ucation.* Granby, Mass.: Bergin and Garvey.

Short, K. G., J. C. Harste, and C. Burke. 1996. *Creating classrooms for authors and in-quirers* (2d ed.). Portsmouth, N.H.: Heinemann.

Shuman, A. 1986. *Storytelling rights: The uses of oral and written texts by urban ado-lescents.* Cambridge: Cambridge University Press.

Silverstein, S. 1981. *A light in the attic.* New York: Harper and Row.

Simon, R. I. 1992. Empowerment as a pedagogy of possibility. In P. Shannon (ed.), *Becoming political: Readings and writings in the politics of literacy education* (pp. 139–51). Portsmouth, N.H.: Heinemann.

Sirotnik, K. A. 1988. What goes on in classrooms? Is this the way we want it? In L. E. Beyer and M. W. Apple (eds.), *The curriculum: Problems, politics, and possibilities* (pp. 56–70). Albany: SUNY Press.

Slapin, B., and D. Seale (eds.). 1992. *Through Indian eyes: The native experience in books for children*. Philadelphia: New Society Publishers.

Sleeter, C. E., and C. A. Grant. 1991. Mapping terrains of power: Student cultural knowledge versus classroom knowledge. In C. E. Sleeter (ed.), *Empowerment through multicultural education* (pp. 49–67). Albany: SUNY Press.

Smith, D. M. 1986. The anthropology of literacy acquisition. In B. B. Schieffelin and P. Gilmore (eds.), *The acquisition of literacy: Ethnographic perspectives* (pp. 261–75). Norwood, N.J.: Ablex.

Smith, F. 1988. *Joining the literacy club: Further essays into education*. Portsmouth, N.H.: Heinemann.

Snauwaert, D. T. 1993. *Democracy, education, and governance: A developmental conception*. Albany: SUNY Press.

Sola, M., and A. T. Bennett. 1985. The struggle for voice: Literacy and consciousness in an East Harlem school. *Journal of Education* 167: 88–110.

Solomon, R. P. 1988. Black cultural forms in schools: A cross national comparison. In L. Weis (ed.), *Class, race, and gender in American education* (pp. 249–65). Albany: SUNY Press.

SooHoo, S., and T. C. Wilson. 1994. Control and contradiction in democratic teacher education: Classroom and curriculum approaches. In J. M. Novak (ed.), *Democratic teacher education: Programs, processes, problems, and prospects* (pp. 163–82). Albany: SUNY Press.

Spears-Bunton, L. A. 1990. Welcome to my house: African American and European American students' responses to Virginia Hamilton's *House of Dies Drear*. *Journal of Negro Education* 59: 566–76.

———. 1996. The miseducation of the American English teacher . . . and getting over it. In R. Powell (ed.), *Multiculturalism and reform: Theoretical perspectives and practical applications* (pp. 51–75). Lexington, Ky.: Institute on Education Reform.

———. 1998. All the colors of the land: A literacy montage. In A. I. Willis (ed.), *Teaching multicultural literature in grades 9–12: Moving beyond the canon* (pp. 17–36). Norwood, Mass.: Christopher-Gordon.

Spring, J. 1991. *American education: An introduction to social and political aspects*. 5th ed. White Plains, N.Y.: Longman.

———. 1994. *Wheels in the head: Educational philosophies of authority, freedom, and culture from Socrates to Paulo Freire*. New York: McGraw-Hill.

Stedman, L. C., and C. F. Kaestle. 1987. Literacy and reading performance in the United States, from 1880 to the present. *Reading Research Quarterly* 22: 8–46.

Stevens, E., Jr., and G. H. Wood. 1992. *Justice, ideology, and education: An introduction to the social foundations of education*. New York: McGraw-Hill.

Street, B. V. 1984. *Literacy in theory and practice*. Cambridge: Cambridge University Press.

———. 1995. *Social literacies: Critical approaches to literacy in development, ethnography, and education*. New York: Longman.

Stumbo, C. 1989. Beyond the classroom. *Harvard Educational Review* 59: 87–97.

Sturk, A. 1992. Developing a community of learners inside and outside the classroom. In P. Shannon (ed.), *Becoming political: Readings and writings in the politics of literacy education* (pp. 263–73). Portsmouth, N.H.: Heinemann.

Susag, D. M. 1998. *Roots and branches: A resource of Native American literature*. Urbana, Ill.: NCTE.

Takaki, R. 1993. *A different mirror: A history of multicultural America*. Boston: Little, Brown and Company.

Taylor, D. 1991. From the child's point of view: Alternate approaches to assessment. In J. A. Roderick (ed.), *Context-responsive approaches to assessing children's language* (pp. 32–51). Urbana, Ill.: NCTE.

Taylor, D., and C. Dorsey-Gaines. 1988. *Growing up literate: Learning from inner-city families*. Portsmouth, N.H.: Heinemann.

Taylor, M. D. 1992. *Mississippi bridge*. New York: Bantam Books.

Tharp, R. G., and R. Gallimore. 1991. *The instructional conversation: Teaching and learning in social activity* (Research Report 2). Santa Cruz: University of California, The National Center for Research on Cultural Diversity and Second Language Learning.

Trafzer, C. 1989. *California's Indians and the Gold Rush*. Newcastle, Calif.: Sierra Oaks.

Uchida, Y. 1982. *Desert exile: The uprooting of a Japanese-American family*. Seattle: University of Washington Press.

Vacha, E. F., and T. F. McLaughlin. 1992. The social, structural, family, school, and personal characteristics of at-risk students. *Journal of Education* 174 (3): 9–25.

Varenne, H., and R. P. McDermott. 1986. "Why" Sheila can read: Structure and indeterminacy in the reproduction of familial literacy. In B. B. Schieffelin and P. Gilmore (eds.), *The acquisition of literacy: Ethnographic perspectives* (pp. 188–210). Norwood, N.J.: Ablex.

Wells, G. 1986. *The meaning makers: Children learning language and using language to learn*. Portsmouth, N.H.: Heinemann.

———. 1988. Developing literate minds. Paper presented at the annual meeting of the American Educational Research Association, New Orleans.

West, C. 1993. *Race matters*. Boston: Beacon Press.

White, J. 1991. *Education and the good life: Autonomy, altruism, and the national curriculum*. New York: Teachers College Press.

Willis, A. I. 1995. Reading the world of school literacy: Contextualizing the experience of a young African American male. *Harvard Educational Review* 65: 30–49.

———. 1998. *Teaching multicultural literature in grades 9–12*. Norwood, Mass.: Christopher-Gordon.

Willis, P. 1977. *Learning to labor*. New York: Columbia University Press.

Wood, G. H. 1988. Democracy and the curriculum. In L. E. Beyer and M. W. Apple (eds.), *The curriculum: Problems, politics, and possibilities* (pp. 166–87). Albany: SUNY Press.

Yep, L. 1993. *Dragon's gate*. New York: HarperCollins Children's Books.

Zaragoza, N. 1997. *Rethinking language arts: Passion and practice*. New York: Garland Publishing.

Zinn, H. 1995. *A people's history of the United States, 1492–present*. New York: HarperCollins Publishers.

# Index

banking model and, 34
counter-hegemonic discourse, 2,
79–80, 87, 93–94, 98, 126
embedded in forms and structures of
schooling, 31, 33, 35
hegemonic forces in society, 105–6,
119
hegemonic functions of language and
literacy, 4, 6, 12–20, 21n1, 25–29,
31, 33, 45, 79–81, 83–87, 91–92,
94–96, 100
Helms, Janet E., 51
Hemingway, Ernest, 88
*Henry IV,* 88
Hiebert, Elfrieda H., 14, 31, 45
Hirsch, E. D., Jr., 18, 35, 44
"Holistic Education in a Prophetic
Voice," 57
holistic theory, 112, 119–21, 124n4 *See
also* whole language
Hollins, Etta R., 44
Holt, Maurice, 29
"Homeless," 113
hooks, bell, 79, 92, 100, 122
Horvath, Barbara M., 26
Hourigan, Maureen M., 95
Houston, Susan H., 26
Hughes, Langston, 102
Hull, Glynda, 14–15, 18
Hymes, Dell, 11–12

*I Know Why the Caged Bird Sings,*
116
ideology
dominant, 20, 24, 33, 44, 51, 54, 85,
94
individualistic, 57, 61–62, 71, 97–98,
107
materialistic, 57, 91–92
objective ways of knowing, 19–20,
30, 32, 36–37, 97–99, 108, 119
positivism, 30, 33, 36
scientific rationality, 29–30, 32,
35–37, 42, 112, 119–22
technological/technocratic rationality, 2–3, 30–31, 37–38, 108
illiteracy, 5, 8, 12, 16–19, 29

productivity and, 14–16 *See also* resistance, student
instructional programs for literacy development
basal reading programs, 31, 47, 114
computer-assisted programs, 31
managed, standardized curricula, 31,
41–46, 48, 53, 55n1
other media and print forms, 67,
72–74, 85–86, 88–92, 96n4, 113–15
textbooks, 32, 34, 40, 42–47, 71,
88–89, 91 *See also* literacy instruction; multicultural/multiethnic
texts, use of

Jackson, Jane, 41
Jefferson, Thomas, 61
Jordan, June, 7–8, 84
Jungck, Susan, 41
justice, 6, 20, 57–59, 63, 75, 90–91, 94,
98–99, 108 *See also* democratic
principles

Kaestel, Carl F., 14
Kane, Jeffrey, 34
Kaye, Harvey J., 60
Keddie, Nell, 27
Keesing, Roger M., 11
Kendrick, Doris M., 108
Kesson, Kathleen, 121
Kiefer, Barbara Z., 9
Kincheloe, Joe L., 30, 36, 42
King, Martin Luther, Jr., 102
knowledge
always partial, 70, 94–95
as a commodity, 34, 87, 97
atomized, 33–34
banking. *See* banking model
control of, 16, 43–46, 49–50
construction versus transmission of,
31, 33–34, 47, 66, 73
cultural/regenerative, 44–45, 47–48,
66, 70, 73, 87, 120
decontextualized, 31–32, 44
linear, 31, 45
meta-knowledge. *See* metalinguistic
knowledge

Shuman, Amy, 25, 28
*Sidewalk Story,* 90
Silberman, Charles, 49
silencing. *See* students, silencing of
Silverstein, Shel, 115
Simon, Roger I., 87, 98
Singer, Isaac Bashevis, 74
Sirotnik, Kenneth A., 50
Slapin, Beverly, 123–24n1
*Slave Dancer, The,* 74
Sleeter, Christine E., 44
Smith, David M., 51
Smith, Frank, 100
socioeconomic status
    drop-out statistics and, 52
    educational failure and, 52, 55n4
    linguistic competence and, 27
    tracking and, 45
speech community, 11–12, 17, 81 *See
    also* discourse, primary
Snauwaert, Dale T., 61, 76n1
Sola, Michele, 37
Soloman, R. Patrick, 29
SooHoo, Suzanne, 118–19
Spears-Bunton, Linda A., 73–74, 101,
    112
Spencer, Kathleen, 44
Spring, Joel, 34, 61
Stedman, Lawrence C., 14
stereotypes, evaluating media and print
    for, 90–91
Stevens, Edward, Jr., 60
Street, Brian V., 16, 32
*Struggle to Continue, The,* 31
students
    as clients, 49–50
    as "objects," 30, 49–50
    as "subjects," 49, 102, 120
    burnout of, 49
    challenging values and beliefs of,
        69–76, 80, 86–96, 118–19
    control of, 43–49, 53–54
    developing communicative compe-
        tence of, 82–86
    passivity of, 6, 28, 46–50, 54, 55n3,
        69, 92, 125

resistance of, 6, 29, 46, 50–53, 55n3,
    55n4, 100, 126–27
silencing voices of, 8, 37, 44, 52, 64,
    66–68, 71, 79–80, 86
Stumbo, Carol, 125–27
Sturk, Audrey, 92, 105
subjective ways of knowing, 19–20, 30,
    112, 119, 121–22
subjectivities, multiple, 70, 93, 96,
    122
Sullivan, William M., 71
Susag, Dorothea M., 124n1
Svendsen, Gro, 73
Swidler, Ann, 71

*tabula rasa,* 30
Takaki, Ronald, 72, 89
"Tanhum," 74
Taylor, Denny, 11, 28, 32, 52
Taylor, Frederick Winslow, 29
Taylor, Mildred, 74
teacher expectations, 27, 48, 96n3
teachers
    as apprentices in acquisition of sec-
        ondary discourses, 82–85
    as transformative intellectuals, 42, 55,
        93–95, 125–27
    challenging values and beliefs of, 68,
        70–71, 76, 93–95
    role of in dialogue, 68–70, 76n4,
        76–77n5, 93
    technical control of, 4, 31, 35–36,
        40–43, 53–54, 95
*Teaching to Transgress,* 79
text reproduction, 47, 66
textbook controversies, 34, 44–45
textbooks. *See* instructional programs
    for literacy development
Tharp, Roland G., 47–48, 66
thematic teaching. *See* literacy instruc-
    tion
Thomas, Piri, 88
*Through Indian Eyes: The Native Ex-
    perience in Books for
    Children,* 123n1
Tipton, Steven M., 71

# About the Author

Rebecca Powell is professor of graduate education at Georgetown College in Georgetown, Kentucky. She is actively involved in several state and national organizations that promote educational equity and has published in numerous books and journals.